AMERICA'S
TEST KITCHEN

also by america's test kitchen

More Mediterranean
The New Cooking School Cookbook: Fundamentals
The Complete Autumn and Winter Cookbook
Five-Ingredient Dinners
One-Hour Comfort
The Ultimate Meal-Prep Cookbook
The Complete Salad Cookbook
The Chicken Bible
Meat Illustrated
Cook for Your Gut Health
The Complete Plant-Based Cookbook
Foolproof Fish
Cooking for One
The Complete One Pot
How Can It Be Gluten-Free Cookbook Collection
The Complete Summer Cookbook
Bowls
Vegetables Illustrated
The Side Dish Bible
100 Techniques
Everything Chocolate
The Perfect Pie
How to Cocktail
Spiced
The Ultimate Burger
The New Essentials Cookbook
Dinner Illustrated
America's Test Kitchen Menu Cookbook
Cook's Illustrated Revolutionary Recipes
Tasting Italy: A Culinary Journey
Cooking at Home with Bridget and Julia
The Complete Mediterranean Cookbook
The Complete Vegetarian Cookbook
The Complete Diabetes Cookbook
The Complete Slow Cooker
The Complete Make-Ahead Cookbook
The Complete Cooking for Two Cookbook
Just Add Sauce
How to Braise Everything
How to Roast Everything
Easy Everyday Keto
Nutritious Delicious
What Good Cooks Know
Cook's Science
The Science of Good Cooking
The Perfect Cake
The Perfect Cookie
Bread Illustrated
Master of the Grill

Kitchen Smarts
Kitchen Hacks
100 Recipes
The New Family Cookbook
The Cook's Illustrated Baking Book
The Cook's Illustrated Cookbook
The America's Test Kitchen Family Baking Book
America's Test Kitchen Twentieth Anniversary
  TV Show Cookbook
The Best of America's Test Kitchen (2007–2022 Editions)
The Complete America's Test Kitchen TV Show
  Cookbook 2001–2022

Healthy and Delicious Instant Pot
Toaster Oven Perfection
Mediterranean Instant Pot
Cook It in Your Dutch Oven
Vegan for Everybody
Sous Vide for Everybody
Air Fryer Perfection
Multicooker Perfection
Food Processor Perfection
Pressure Cooker Perfection
Instant Pot Ace Blender Cookbook
Naturally Sweet
Foolproof Preserving
Paleo Perfected
The Best Mexican Recipes
Slow Cooker Revolution Volume 2: The Easy-Prep Edition
Slow Cooker Revolution
The America's Test Kitchen D.I.Y. Cookbook

THE COOK'S ILLUSTRATED ALL-TIME BEST SERIES
All-Time Best Brunch
All-Time Best Dinners for Two
All-Time Best Sunday Suppers
All-Time Best Holiday Entertaining
All-Time Best Soups

COOK'S COUNTRY TITLES
Big Flavors from Italian America
One-Pan Wonders
Cook It in Cast Iron
Cook's Country Eats Local
The Complete Cook's Country TV Show Cookbook

FOR A FULL LISTING OF ALL OUR BOOKS
CooksIllustrated.com
AmericasTestKitchen.com

praise for america's test kitchen titles

"Cooking inspiration: Enjoy 100 recipes, ranging from mini meatloaves to a whole chicken."
READERSDIGEST.COM ON *TOASTER OVEN PERFECTION*

"The book's depth, breadth, and practicality makes it a must-have for seafood lovers."
PUBLISHERS WEEKLY* (STARRED REVIEW) ON *FOOLPROOF FISH

"Another flawless entry in the America's Test Kitchen canon, *Bowls* guides readers of all culinary skill levels in composing one-bowl meals from a variety of cuisines."
BUZZFEED BOOKS ON *BOWLS*

"If there's room in the budget for one multicooker/Instant Pot cookbook, make it this one."
BOOKLIST ON *MULTICOOKER PERFECTION*

"This book upgrades slow cooking for discriminating, 21st century palates—that is indeed revolutionary."
THE DALLAS MORNING NEWS* ON *SLOW COOKER REVOLUTION

"This book begins with a detailed buying guide, a critical summary of available sizes and attachments, and a list of clever food processor techniques. Easy and versatile dishes follow . . . Both new and veteran food processor owners will love this practical guide."
LIBRARY JOURNAL* ON *FOOD PROCESSOR PERFECTION

Selected as the Cookbook Award Winner of 2019 in the Health and Special Diet Category
INTERNATIONAL ASSOCIATION OF CULINARY PROFESSIONALS (IACP) ON *THE COMPLETE DIABETES COOKBOOK*

"The book offers an impressive education for curious cake makers, new and experienced alike. A summation of 25 years of cake making at ATK, there are cakes for every taste."
THE WALL STREET JOURNAL* ON *THE PERFECT CAKE

"*The Perfect Cookie* . . . is, in a word, perfect. This is an important and substantial cookbook . . . If you love cookies, but have been a tad shy to bake on your own, all your fears will be dissipated. This is one book you can use for years with magnificently happy results."
THE HUFFINGTON POST* ON *THE PERFECT COOKIE

"If you're a home cook who loves long introductions that tell you why a dish works followed by lots of step-by-step hand holding, then you'll love *Vegetables Illustrated*."
THE WALL STREET JOURNAL* ON *VEGETABLES ILLUSTRATED

"True to its name, this smart and endlessly enlightening cookbook is about as definitive as it's possible to get in the modern vegetarian realm."
MEN'S JOURNAL* ON *THE COMPLETE VEGETARIAN COOKBOOK

"A one-volume kitchen seminar, addressing in one smart chapter after another the sometimes surprising whys behind a cook's best practices . . . You get the myth, the theory, the science, and the proof, all rigorously interrogated as only America's Test Kitchen can do."
NPR ON *THE SCIENCE OF GOOD COOKING*

"The 21st-century *Fannie Farmer Cookbook* or *The Joy of Cooking*. If you had to have one cookbook and that's all you could have, this one would do it."
CBS SAN FRANCISCO ON *THE NEW FAMILY COOKBOOK*

"Some 2,500 photos walk readers through 600 painstakingly tested recipes, leaving little room for error."
ASSOCIATED PRESS ON *THE AMERICA'S TEST KITCHEN COOKING SCHOOL COOKBOOK*

"The go-to gift book for newlyweds, small families, or empty nesters."
ORLANDO SENTINEL* ON *THE COMPLETE COOKING FOR TWO COOKBOOK

"Some books impress by the sheer audacity of their ambition. Backed by the magazine's famed mission to test every recipe relentlessly until it is the best it can be, this nearly 900-page volume lands with an authoritative wallop."
CHICAGO TRIBUNE* ON *THE COOK'S ILLUSTRATED COOKBOOK

"It might become your 'cooking school,' the only book you'll need to make you a proficient cook, recipes included . . . You can master the 100 techniques with the easy-to-understand instructions, then apply the skill with the recipes that follow."
THE LITCHFIELD COUNTY TIMES* ON *100 TECHNIQUES

HEALTHY
AIR FRYER

75 FEEL-GOOD RECIPES. ANY MEAL. ANY AIR FRYER.

AMERICA'S TEST KITCHEN

Library of Congress Cataloging-in-Publication Data

Names: America's Test Kitchen (Firm), author.

Title: Healthy air fryer : 75 feel-good recipes, any meal any air fryer / America's Test Kitchen.

Description: Boston : America's Test Kitchen, [2022] | Includes index.

Identifiers: LCCN 2021045827 (print) | LCCN 2021045828 (ebook) | ISBN 9781948703901 (paperback) | ISBN 9781948703918 (ebook)

Subjects: LCSH: Hot air frying. | LCGFT: Cookbooks.

Classification: LCC TX689 .H44 2022 (print) | LCC TX689 (ebook) | DDC 641.7/7--dc23

LC record available at https://lccn.loc.gov/2021045827

LC ebook record available at https://lccn.loc.gov/2021045828

America's Test Kitchen
21 Drydock Avenue, Boston, MA 02210

Printed in Canada

10 9 8 7 6 5 4 3 2 1

Distributed by Penguin Random House Publisher Services
Tel: 800.733.3000

Pictured on front cover: CRISPY PORK CHOPS WITH ROASTED PEACH, BLACKBERRY, AND ARUGULA SALAD (PAGE 84), OVERNIGHT BREAKFAST GRAIN BOWL (PAGE 31), SPICED CHICKEN KEBABS WITH VEGETABLE AND BULGUR SALAD (PAGE 58), SALMON BURGERS WITH TOMATO CHUTNEY (PAGE 102), ROASTED DELICATA SQUASH (PAGE 147), ROMESCO (PAGE 169)

Pictured on back cover: ASPARAGUS FRIES WITH YOGURT SAUCE (PAGE 162), CORIANDER CHICKEN THIGHS WITH ROASTED CAULIFLOWER AND SHALLOTS (PAGE 56), ROASTED BROCCOLI (PAGE 131), HONEY-GLAZED SALMON WITH SNAP PEAS AND RADISHES (PAGE 98), TOP SIRLOIN STEAK WITH ROASTED ZUCCHINI AND SHIITAKES (PAGE 76), EGG IN A HOLE WITH TOMATO, AVOCADO, AND HERB SALAD (PAGE 16)

Editorial Director, Books ADAM KOWIT

Executive Food Editor DAN ZUCCARELLO

Deputy Food Editor STEPHANIE PIXLEY

Executive Managing Editor DEBRA HUDAK

Senior Editors NICOLE KONSTANTINAKOS AND KAUMUDI MARATHÉ

Associate Editor SAMANTHA BLOCK

Additional Recipe Development GARTH CLINGINGSMITH AND REBECCAH MARSTERS

Assistant Editor EMILY RAHRAVAN

Design Director LINDSEY TIMKO CHANDLER

Associate Art Director ASHLEY TENN

Photography Director JULIE BOZZO COTE

Photography Producer MEREDITH MULCAHY

Senior Staff Photographers STEVE KLISE AND DANIEL J. VAN ACKERE

Staff Photographer KEVIN WHITE

Additional Photography NINA GALLANT, JOSEPH KELLER, AND CARL TREMBLAY

Food Styling JOY HOWARD, CATRINE KELTY, CHANTAL LAMBETH, KENDRA MCNIGHT, ASHLEY MOORE, CHRISTIE MORRISON, ELLE SIMONE SCOTT, KENDRA SMITH

Photoshoot Kitchen Team

Photo Team and Special Events Manager ALLISON BERKEY

Lead Test Cook ERIC HAESSLER

Test Cooks HANNAH FENTON, JACQUELINE GOCHENOUER, AND GINA MCCREADIE

Assistant Test Cooks HISHAM HASSAN AND CHRISTA WEST

Senior Manager, Publishing Operations TAYLOR ARGENZIO

Imaging Manager LAUREN ROBBINS

Production and Imaging Specialists TRICIA NEUMYER, DENNIS NOBLE, AND AMANDA YONG

Lead Copy Editor RACHEL SCHOWALTER

Copy Editor APRIL POOLE

Proofreader VICKI ROWLAND

Indexer ELIZABETH PARSON

Chief Creative Officer JACK BISHOP

Executive Editorial Directors JULIA COLLIN DAVISON AND BRIDGET LANCASTER

CONTENTS

ix   Welcome to America's Test Kitchen

x   Getting Started

14   **Breakfast**

36   **Poultry**

70   **Beef and Pork**

94   **Seafood**

118   **Vegetable Mains and Sides**

148   **Small Bites**

176   Conversions and Equivalents

177   Index

WELCOME TO AMERICA'S TEST KITCHEN

This book has been tested, written, and edited by the folks at America's Test Kitchen, where curious cooks become confident cooks. Located in Boston's Seaport District in the historic Innovation and Design Building, it features 15,000 square feet of kitchen space including multiple photography and video studios. It is the home of *Cook's Illustrated* magazine and *Cook's Country* magazine and is the workday destination for more than 60 test cooks, editors, and cookware specialists. Our mission is to empower and inspire confidence, community, and creativity in the kitchen.

We start the process of testing a recipe with a complete lack of preconceptions, which means that we accept no claim, no technique, and no recipe at face value. We simply assemble as many variations as possible, test a half-dozen of the most promising, and taste the results blind. We then construct our own recipe and continue to test it, varying ingredients, techniques, and cooking times until we reach a consensus. As we like to say in the test kitchen, "We make the mistakes so you don't have to." The result, we hope, is the best version of a particular recipe, but we realize that only you can be the final judge of our success (or failure). We use the same rigorous approach when we test equipment and taste ingredients.

All of this would not be possible without a belief that good cooking, much like good music, is based on a foundation of objective technique. Some people like spicy foods and others don't, but there is a right way to sauté, there is a best way to cook a pot roast, and there are measurable scientific principles involved in producing perfectly beaten, stable egg whites. Our ultimate goal is to investigate the fundamental principles of cooking to give you the techniques, tools, and ingredients you need to become a better cook. It is as simple as that.

To see what goes on behind the scenes at America's Test Kitchen, check out our social media channels for kitchen snapshots, exclusive content, video tips, and much more. You can watch us work (in our actual test kitchen) by tuning in to *America's Test Kitchen* or *Cook's Country* on public television or on our websites. Listen to *Proof, Mystery Recipe*, and *The Walk-In* (AmericasTestKitchen.com/podcasts) to hear engaging, complex stories about people and food. Want to hone your cooking skills or finally learn how to bake—with an America's Test Kitchen test cook? Enroll in one of our online cooking classes. And you can engage the next generation of home cooks with kid-tested recipes from America's Test Kitchen Kids.

Our community of home recipe testers provides valuable feedback on recipes under development by ensuring that they are foolproof. You can help us investigate the how and why behind successful recipes from your home kitchen. (Sign up at AmericasTestKitchen.com/recipe_testing.)

However you choose to visit us, we welcome you into our kitchen, where you can stand by our side as we test our way to the best recipes in America.

---

 facebook.com/AmericasTestKitchen

 instagram.com/TestKitchen

 youtube.com/AmericasTestKitchen

 tiktok.com/@TestKitchen

 twitter.com/TestKitchen

 pinterest.com/TestKitchen

AmericasTestKitchen.com
CooksIllustrated.com
CooksCountry.com
OnlineCookingSchool.com
AmericasTestKitchen.com/kids

GETTING STARTED

1 Introduction

2 Ten Ways to Eat Healthy
Using the Air Fryer

4 Go Way Beyond Frying

5 Tips and Techniques for Success

6 The Four Styles of Air Fryer We Used

8 Rating Drawer- and Oven-Style
Air Fryers

10 Scaling Our Recipes

11 Handy Equipment to Use with
Your Air Fryer

12 Simple Uses for Your Air Fryer

INTRODUCTION

If you want to make the most of your air fryer every day and eat healthier while doing so, you've come to the right place. In *Healthy Air Fryer*, you'll find food that tastes great; looks great; and, best of all, is good for you.

We're big fans of air fryers for their convenience, speed, and consistent results. We learned from our first book, *Air Fryer Perfection*, that their benefits go well beyond frying with less oil. Here, we push the limits again by showing more ways the air fryer can simplify healthy eating, from morning to night.

Our test cooks went back into the kitchen and used the air fryer to make hearty breakfasts, mouthwatering lunchtime salads and noodle bowls, and vibrant dinners. They cooked mounds of vegetables to learn how to get the best results in the air fryer's intense heat, whether cooking kale, sweet potatoes, or bok choy. They turned to healthy pantry ingredients such as yogurt and nuts to create tantalizing flavors (like a pistachio crust for salmon), roasted fruits to jazz up simple meals (try the Crispy Pork Chops with Roasted Peach, Blackberry, and Arugula Salad [page 96]), and incorporated an array of spices and condiments.

Some of the most exciting dishes came from experimenting with an ovensafe bowl or soufflé dish and a round cake pan, which opened up a world of baking liquid-y dishes. Now we could bake eggs or porridge and eat them from the same bowl (no pot to wash). We loved how a 6-inch cake pan produced a well-browned vegetable frittata that was perfectly sized for two. The cake pan also came in handy for one-dish dinners, such as turkey meatballs in tomato sauce, and a saucy white bean and mushroom gratin.

Everyone enjoyed baking up a storm of whole grain–enriched baked goods such as whole-wheat muffins, oat scones that can be baked individually from frozen, trail mix, and even Apple Crisp (page 13).

Of course, dinner is still the main event, and here our test cooks sought to balance moderate portions of meat, chicken, and fish with ample servings of vegetables. Often, success came from stacking ingredients so that everything cooked together, with the meat and fish juices flavoring the vegetables below in dishes such as Chicken Thighs with Roasted Mushrooms and Tomatoes (page 55). We also developed some stellar vegetable mains, including the perfect air-fryer veggie burger, and upped our salad game by browning halloumi cheese and roasting butternut squash to feature in a deeply satisfying main-dish salad.

Speaking of crispy, it wouldn't be air-frying if we didn't bring the crispy and crunchy elements. You'll find supercrispy shoestring fries, thanks to spiralized potatoes; egg rolls; extra-crisp chicken wings made without any additional fat; and hand pies made with store-bought phyllo dough that becomes shatteringly crisp in the air fryer.

Last but not least, we tested every recipe in multiple styles and models of air fryers to make sure that they would work in any air fryer, new or old. That's how we can say our air-fryer recipes are foolproof, no matter what kind of machine you have.

So let's get air-frying. Whether it's breakfast, lunch, dinner, or snack time, your air fryer and the following recipes are waiting for you.

TEN WAYS TO EAT HEALTHY USING THE AIR FRYER

Of course you know that air fryers fry with less oil. But there are other creative ways they help you to eat healthier. Here are 10 of them.

1 Hands-Off Breakfasts Eating a healthy and hearty breakfast at home often falls by the wayside, but our easy recipes help you turn out a hot breakfast that's ready when you are. Cook perfect eggs with savory vegetables or whole-grain porridge in an ovensafe bowl right in the air fryer and then conveniently eat out of it (minimizing cleanup). Or bake a cheese-and-vegetable-stuffed frittata for two using a cake pan. You can save time and prep parts of many recipes ahead as well as make and freeze breakfast burritos and fruit-and-nut oat scones for mornings when you need to grab and go.

2 Vegetable-Forward Dinners To build a healthy dinner, we pair a larger quantity of deliciously roasted vegetables with a more moderate portion of leaner protein. Strategically stacking ingredients to cook on top of each other, sometimes at staggered times, lets the meat or fish juices season the vegetables below and allows the components to finish cooking at the same time. The hot air circulates between ingredients so that they cook evenly, while stacking them prevents them from sticking to each other and turning soggy.

3 New Ideas for Vegetables We use a great variety of vegetables, from green beans and delicata squash to eggplant, mushrooms, and napa cabbage kimchi, treating them more inventively than ever. We use them raw in interesting salads, like the brussels sprouts in Chipotle-Honey Fried Chicken with Brussels Sprout and Citrus Salad (page 50); turn them into breakfast in Hearty Vegetable Hash with Golden Yogurt (page 27); cook them for dips, like the tomatoes and garlic in Romesco (page 169); and use them in a filling for savory Make-Ahead Phyllo Hand Pies (page 158).

4 Foolproof Fish Using an air fryer prevents fish from getting overcooked, tough, or dry all without hovering over the stove. Put in your protein, set the timer, and go on with the rest of your cooking knowing you'll get tender, perfectly cooked fish and shellfish every time. Try Crispy Halibut with Leafy Greens and Tartar Sauce (page 106), Pistachio-Crusted Salmon (page 96), Ginger-Turmeric Scallops with Mango and Cucumber Salad (page 110), and more.

7 Healthier Snacks If you're looking for healthier snacks and small bites, we've got you covered. Instead of opening up a bag of chips, make our supersimple Almond, Cherry, and Chocolate Trail Mix (page 174) or protein-packed Crispy Barbecue Chickpeas (page 170). For heartier satisfaction, try appetizers such as Beef-and-Bulgur Meatballs with Tahini-Yogurt Dipping Sauce (page 154) and three flavors of crisp chicken wings (page 150). The fat drips away, so you can feel good about making wings that are delicious but leaner than the usual fried ones.

8 Roast Fruit Roasting enhances the sweetness of fruit without the addition of sugar and turns it tender. The benefit of the air fryer is quick roasting, so you can incorporate fruit more often. We roasted peaches for a fruit-filled savory salad to pair with crispy pork chops (page 84) and added a roasted pineapple salsa to our chicken-tomatillo tacos (page 64). And when you want a treat, there's Roasted Fruit Topping (page 12), which you could put on yogurt or cereal, toast, or frozen yogurt or ice cream.

9 Bring the Grill Indoors "Air grilling" is a naturally healthy way to cook since little to no oil is used. The high heat of the air fryer makes it supereasy to add beautiful char to both meat and vegetables all year long in dishes such as Spiced Chicken Kebabs with Vegetable and Bulgur Salad (page 58).

5 Better Salads Though it seems counterintuitive to use your air fryer to make salads, you can not only assemble a traditional salad while your meal air-fries but also air-fry ingredients to add a roasted, crunchy component to your salad. For Hoisin-Ginger Chicken Salad with Napa Cabbage, Shiitakes, and Bell Pepper (page 62), we air-fry shiitakes underneath the chicken. For Spicy Roasted Shrimp and Fennel Salad with Cannellini Beans and Watercress (page 112), we air-fry both the shrimp and the fennel before mixing them with the other ingredients.

10 Perfect Portions The compact size of the air fryer is perfect for cooking smaller servings. Our recipes are scaled down and so flavorful that eating in moderation is easy and satisfying. We kept protein portions to 4 to 6 ounces and included larger servings of fiber-rich vegetables in our complete meals. For the protein-only recipes, pair them with one or more of the many appealing vegetable sides.

6 Whole-Grain Baking Professional bakers have long relied on the even heat of convection ovens. Now you can use your air fryer to bake with success. Try making whole grain–enriched Whole-Wheat Blueberry-Almond Muffins (page 35), Make-Ahead Fruit, Nut, and Oat Scones (page 32), and a fruit-filled Apple Crisp (page 13).

GO WAY BEYOND FRYING

Despite its name, the air fryer is really a convection oven. While often used to fry with little oil or to cook frozen french fries, we learned it can be used successfully to roast proteins, vegetables, and fruit and also to bake, warm, toast, and "pan"-fry.

Great Frying, Superior Roasting

We love to fry in the air fryer, but we capitalized on the fact that the air fryer really excels at air-roasting, a pretty healthy way to cook. Because of the way the appliance works (with a hot coil at the top and a fan circulating even heat around the inside), we could achieve really uniform cooking and great browning on all kinds of protein: chicken breasts, pork chops, salmon fillets, and more. Every protein remained surprisingly juicy. We also roasted a wide variety of vegetables and fruit.

Inventive, Complete Meals

We started to think of the air fryer as the appliance and its basket as a vessel. With that mindset, we got creative with one-dish cooking, cooking a protein and vegetable(s) at the same time. Strategically stacking the components on top of each other allows not only the heat to circulate on all sides but also lets the juices from the meat or fish on top flavor the vegetables underneath. Plus, it's very convenient to have a whole meal ready at the same time. We cooked chicken thighs on mushrooms and tomatoes for our take on cacciatore, pork tenderloin over green beans, and pieces of haddock on top of brussels sprouts, to name just a few recipes.

Container Cooking

While trying to figure out how to incorporate wet ingredients into our recipes, we realized that we didn't need to be limited to just the air-fryer basket. Using ovensafe vessels that fit into the basket—such as a bowl, soufflé dish, or non-stick cake pan—to hold liquid-y items was a revelation and really expanded the range of dishes we could cook in our air fryer. We baked eggs and porridge for breakfast in bowls we could then eat out of, cooked saucy pasta and meatballs as well as salmon and braised kimchi in a cake pan for dinner, and developed a recipe for individual apple crisp for dessert.

From Your Fridge or Freezer in a Flash

The air fryer excels at crisping up frozen foods, so it's great for cooking premade items for breakfast, dinner, and appetizers. This batch of recipes can be made ahead and frozen:

- Make-Ahead Breakfast Burritos (page 24)
- Make-Ahead Fruit, Nut, and Oat Scones (page 32)
- Make-Ahead Lentil and Mushroom Burgers (page 128)
- Make-Ahead Crispy Egg Rolls (page 156)
- Make-Ahead Phyllo Hand Pies with Fennel, Olive, and Goat Cheese Filling (page 158)

TIPS AND TECHNIQUES FOR SUCCESS

While air fryers are really easy to use, you have to do a little more than just turn them on and walk away. Here are some tips, tricks, and techniques that will help you get the most out of your air fryer.

Better Browning

While cooking in the air fryer is low fat, it isn't no fat. A little fat promotes superlative browning and can help food crisp up. We spray or brush meat and fish with canola oil (spraying makes it easy to focus the oil on top of the protein). Fat isn't the only way to boost browning. Glazes using honey, preserves, and hoisin sauce all add flavor, and they also help food brown.

Skewer It

Threading pieces of chicken or vegetables onto wooden skewers provides an easy way to space food out in the basket and maximize air exposure. It also helps generate some flavorful charring.

"LINCOLN LOG" YOUR SKEWERS AND VEGETABLES

For easy multilayered cooking, arrange half the skewers or vegetable pieces in the basket, spaced evenly apart. Arrange the remaining skewers or vegetables on top, perpendicular to the first layer, log cabin–style.

Add a Little Water

Roasting can dry out some vegetables such as leeks, so our trick is to add a little water to the base of the drawer. The water evaporates while the vegetables steam-roast, giving them added moisture.

MAKING AN ALUMINUM FOIL SLING

1 Fold one long sheet of foil so that it is 4 inches wide. Lay the sheet of foil widthwise across the basket or rack. Press the foil up and into the sides and fold any excess foil as needed so that the edges of the foil are flush with the lip of the basket.

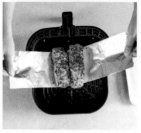

2 After cooking, use the sling to carefully remove the fish from the air-fryer basket.

A Word About Preheating

A few newer models—including our winner—recommend preheating to ensure that the frying basket is hot when the food touches it. Some air fryers have automatic preheating times and presets indicating when to add or turn food. We found preheating unnecessary. To allow for differences across models, the cooking times in our recipes are meant to be counted as soon as you press "start."

Forget About Attachments

Some air fryers come with rotisserie baskets (barrel-shaped mesh cages) or frying baskets with auto-stir attachments. These accessories are designed to agitate the food, thus eliminating the need for manually shaking the baskets midcook, a common air fryer requirement. But they are fussy to use and don't make better food.

THE FOUR STYLES OF AIR FRYER WE USED

WINNER

DRAWER

A drawer-style air fryer has an easy-to-use basket that slides into the appliance in a drawer. The basket has one wide cooking surface and sits on a plastic or metal tray that catches crumbs and excess oil and drippings. A single large, stay-cool handle allows you to maneuver the basket easily and to shake it to redistribute the food in it partway through cooking. Our winning air fryer, the **Instant Vortex Plus 6-Quart Air Fryer**, is a drawer-style model.

PROS:

- We can't say enough good things about the drawer-style model of air fryer; it's the gold standard and by far our favorite to use. The basket acts like a vessel, and the enclosed space allows for the best layering of ingredients.

- No matter the size, drawer-style air fryers have the most real estate for cooking. We prefer one cooking surface to multiple racks.

CONS:

- None

INSTANT POT LID

Instant Pot makes a lid with a heating element that locks into place on certain Instant Pot multicookers, turning the multicooker into an air fryer. Inserts include two baskets with perforated bottoms that sit one on top of the other, but we don't recommend cooking with both baskets at the same time (we used only the upper basket).

PROS:

- The lid did well with all our recipes. You can roast a whole chicken with it if you remove the insert.

- A lid is a convenient option if you are trying to avoid having another whole appliance.

CONS:

- Its cooking space is limited, so it is harder to make doubled versions of recipes.

- There are no heatproof handles, so you need oven mitts or tongs to take out the baskets.

OVEN

The oven-style air fryer is designed like an oven, with two racks and a door that opens outward. The multiple cooking racks and baskets don't have handles, and their perforations allow crumbs and drips to fall through onto the oven base, or worse, the floor. The upper rack blocks heat from reaching the lower one, resulting in unevenly cooked food, even if you move and rotate the racks partway through cooking.

PRO:

- Even though this style has less space for cooking, it is able to handle large roasts well.

CONS:

- Don't be fooled by the 10-quart capacity: It has less space for cooking than a 6-quart drawer-style air fryer.

- The racks make stacking ingredients more challenging.

TOASTER OVEN

Some toaster ovens now have an air-frying function. Good for kitchens with limited counter space, air-fryer toaster ovens are larger than drawer-style air fryers and can accommodate more food. But these ovens often cook food slower than other air fryers, and many need preheating. Our test kitchen favorite is the **Breville Smart Oven Air**.

PRO:

- If you are trying to maximize the potential of your appliances, then this model is a smart choice. This model is also good if you want to cook traditional sheet-pan meals and other foods such as cookies that require a sheet pan.

CONS:

- Air-fryer toaster ovens are generally more expensive than other styles of air fryer.

- Some models have a fan located on the side, making rotating the hot handleless tray essential for even browning.

highly recommended	performance	comments

Instant
Vortex Plus 6-Quart Air Fryer

WINNER

MODEL n/a
PRICE $119.95
STYLE Drawer
CONTROLS Digital
HEIGHT 12.5 in

COOKING ★★★
SAFETY ★★★
CAPACITY ★★★
EASE OF USE ★★½

Our winning air fryer delivers on its promise of an extra-large capacity. Though it's only about a foot tall, it was large enough to fit four chicken cutlets or two 15-ounce bags of frozen french fries, cooking everything to crispy, golden perfection. We were even able to cook a whole 4-pound chicken in it. A quick, 2-minute preheat ensured that the interior was hot when we added food. The wide drawer-style basket was easy to remove and insert—and our hands were safeguarded from the heating element—and its sturdy handle allowed us to shake its contents for easy redistribution. Intuitive digital controls were brightly lit and easy to operate. This fryer is a great option for a family of four or anyone looking for more cooking space without adding much bulk.

Philips
Premium Airfryer with
Fat Removal Technology

MODEL HD9741/99
PRICE $219.95
STYLE Drawer
CONTROLS Digital
HEIGHT 11 in

COOKING ★★★
SAFETY ★★★
CAPACITY ★★
EASE OF USE ★★★

We love this machine's slim, compact footprint and the fact that its nonstick cooking basket was easy to clean and had a removable bottom for deeper cleaning. Its digital controls and dial-operated menu made setting the time and temperature intuitive. It automatically stopped cooking as soon as the set time was up, and its drawer allowed us to remove its cooking basket without exposing our hands to the heating element. It can't hold as much food as our winner, but it can handle small batches of frozen foods or recipes intended to serve two people.

recommended	performance	comments

GoWISE USA
3.7-Quart 7-in-1 Air Fryer

BEST BUY

MODEL GW22621
PRICE $75.15
STYLE Drawer
CONTROLS Digital
HEIGHT 13 in

COOKING ★★★
SAFETY ★★★
CAPACITY ★★
EASE OF USE ★★½

This air fryer's digital controls weren't as intuitive as those of our favorite models, but it was still easy to set the time and temperature once we got the hang of the buttons. It cooked foods quickly, and its display was bright, large, and easy to read. Its drawer and automatic shutoff were a boon to safety, and its non-stick interior was easy to clean. Its small capacity wouldn't work for a crowd, but it cooked our recipes for two and small batches of frozen fries without issue.

Philips
Premium Analog Airfryer

MODEL HD9721/99
PRICE $199.95
STYLE Drawer
CONTROLS Analog
HEIGHT 11.2 in

COOKING ★★★
SAFETY ★★★
CAPACITY ★★
EASE OF USE ★★

This model's small stature and footprint make it easy to store, but it's large enough to cook small batches of frozen foods and our recipes evenly and quickly. Its nonstick interior was easy to clean, but its analog temperature and timer dials weren't as precise as digital controls.

recommended (cont.)

	performance	comments

Rosewill
RHAF-15004 1400W Oil-Less
Low Fat Air Fryer - 3.3-Quart
(3.2L), Black

MODEL RHAF-15004
PRICE $60.20
STYLE Drawer
CONTROLS Analog
HEIGHT 12 in

COOKING ★★★
SAFETY ★★★
CAPACITY ★★
EASE OF USE ★★

Another smaller, drawer-style air fryer that fits easily under cabinets, this analog model had simple, intuitive controls. It cooked food well and cleaned up easily, but testers struggled when sliding the basket into the machine, and the basket required some jiggering to lock in. As with other analog models, its temperature dial was less precise, and it was easy to knock slightly away from the target temperature.

recommended with reservations

	performance	comments

Kalorik
AirFryer with Dual Layer Rack

MODEL FT 42139 BK
PRICE $89.99
STYLE Drawer
CONTROLS Analog
HEIGHT 13 in

COOKING ★★★
SAFETY ★★★
CAPACITY ★★
EASE OF USE ★

This basic analog model was compact and easy to use, but its timer stopped working early on, forcing us to use an alternate timer. It comes with a one-year warranty, but the company was unresponsive to calls and messages left with the warranty line. A subsequent model we tried didn't have this problem and made crispy, crunchy food.

GoWISE USA
8-in-1 XL 5.8QT Air Fryer

MODEL GW22731
PRICE $99.95
STYLE Drawer
CONTROLS Digital
HEIGHT 11.5 in

COOKING ★★
SAFETY ★★★
CAPACITY ★★
EASE OF USE ★★

This model took up more counter space than its 3.7-quart counterpart. Its cooking basket was a bit deeper, but its cooking surface was only about ½ inch wider, and there wasn't enough room to cook double batches of recipes. When we tried making two bags of frozen french fries, they were undercooked, with the fries toward the center being flabby and raw, despite frequent tossing during cooking. Still, this model cooked single batches as well as the smaller version.

Instant
Vortex Plus 10-quart
Air Fryer Oven

MODEL n/a
PRICE $119.00
STYLE Oven
CONTROLS Digital
HEIGHT 14 in

COOKING ★★
SAFETY ★★
CAPACITY ★★
EASE OF USE ★½

Our hopes for an easy-to-use oven-style model were dashed with this air fryer. The instructions suggest using the rotisserie basket to cook fries and other small foods, but this accessory was frustrating to open, fill, close, insert, and remove, especially when the metal was hot. The cramped interior did little to ensure even cooking. We had better results when we prepared small batches of fries on the perforated oven-style racks. However, when we tried doubling a chicken recipe and used two racks, the cutlets cooked unevenly.

GoWISE USA
Vibe 11.6 qt. Air Fryer

MODEL GW77722
PRICE $119.99
STYLE Oven
CONTROLS Digital
HEIGHT 5 in

COOKING ★★
SAFETY ★★
CAPACITY ★★
EASE OF USE ★½

Despite touting an 11.6-quart capacity, this model couldn't really handle much more food than smaller drawer-style air fryers. Single layers of food cooked evenly and quickly, crisping up nicely, but food on the upper rack blocked heat from reaching the lower rack, resulting in uneven cooking. The metal racks trapped cheese and molasses and were tedious to clean.

MODELS TESTED AND NOT RECOMMENDED: Black+Decker 2 Liter Purifry Air Fryer, Chefman Turbofry Air Oven with Auto-Stir Function, Elite Platinum Electric Digital Air Fryer, De'Longhi Multifry, Gourmia FreeFry 360 TurboXP Cookcenter

SCALING OUR RECIPES

To accommodate the widest variety of air fryers, we developed most of the recipes in this book to serve two. That said, many of the recipes can be easily scaled up to serve more people.

Doubling a Recipe

If a recipe can be doubled, we indicate this in the headnote of the recipe. If you are doubling a recipe, double all the ingredients.

If your air fryer has a capacity of 6 quarts or more, you can double a recipe and still cook it in a single batch. However, it is critical to leave enough room for air circulation around the ingredients to ensure even cooking. If you have a smaller air fryer (less than 6 quarts) and are doubling a recipe, you will need to cook in batches.

Scaling Proteins

For some stand-alone proteins such as salmon fillets and bone-in chicken breasts, the recipes offer the flexibility to cook one to four pieces, as indicated in the yield line. Here, again, be sure to leave space for the air to circulate around each piece. The number you'll be able to fit depends on the size of your air fryer; a smaller air fryer holds two pieces of fish or chicken. If a recipe calls for doubling steaks, use two steaks of the same size instead of one bigger steak.

Cooking Times

For a few recipes, such as Hearty Vegetable Hash with Golden Yogurt (page 27), a longer cooking time may be needed when doubling it. If that is the case, the increased time is listed in the recipe headnote.

Vessel Inserts

Ovensafe vessels work well in the air fryer to cook liquid-y ingredients (see page 4 for more information). Before you fill any vessel with ingredients, make sure that it fits in your air fryer.

DOUBLE IT

3-cup ovensafe bowl
Serves 1

1½-quart soufflé dish
Serves 2

HANDY EQUIPMENT TO USE
WITH YOUR AIR FRYER

Ovensafe Bowl, Soufflé Dish, and Ramekin

We use a 3-cup (24-ounce) ovensafe bowl (which then can be conveniently eaten out of) or 1½-quart soufflé dish in many recipes to hold and cook wet or liquid-y ingredients in the air fryer. For individual portions of dessert, a 6-ounce ramekin works great.

6-Inch Round Nonstick or Silicone Cake Pan

Experimenting with a 6-inch nonstick cake pan opened up exciting new recipe possibilities since it allowed us to use liquid-y ingredients such as eggs for a frittata, tomato sauce for meatballs, and kimchi. We also used this pan to bake our snack bars. It's easy to put in and take out of the air fryer when hot; we recommend using tongs in one hand and an oven mitt on the other to help with that.

Aluminum Foil or Silicone Muffin-Tin Liners

Our test cooks found that both aluminum foil and silicone liners worked equally well when making muffins in the air fryer.

6-Inch Wooden Skewers

We use 6-inch wooden skewers to make chicken and vegetable kebabs. This length fits into any size air fryer.

Nonstick-Safe Spatula

Since many air-fryer baskets and inserts have a nonstick coating, we use a nonstick-safe spatula to retrieve cooked fish and more out of the air fryer. We especially like the long, narrow head of the **Matfer Bourgeat Exoglass Pelton Spatula**.

Kitchen Tongs

A good pair of tongs serves many a purpose in the kitchen. They are great for placing, moving, and tossing ingredients in the air fryer and are particularly helpful for lifting hot ramekins and cake pans out of the air fryer. Our favorite kitchen tongs are the **OXO Good Grips 12-Inch Tongs**.

Oven Mitts

Oven mitts are essential for keeping your hands protected when handling hot parts of the air fryer or pans or bowls inside. Our grip was secure even on the small handles or knobs on an air fryer when using our winning oven mitt, the heavily textured **OXO Silicone Oven Mitt**.

Oil Mister

For a sustainable alternative to canned oil spray, you can use a refillable oil mister. We frequently spray the air-fryer basket to prevent sticking and spray ingredients such as chicken and pork to keep them moist and help with browning. We like to keep one mister filled with canola oil and another with olive oil, using the **Norpro Hard Plastic and Stainless Steel Sprayer Mister**.

Aluminum Foil

We use aluminum foil to tent meat while it rests and to wrap foods before freezing. We also use it sometimes to line the air-fryer basket and to make a foil sling (see page 5) to help lift delicate fish out of the air fryer so that it doesn't break apart.

SIMPLE USES FOR YOUR AIR FRYER

Toast Chiles, Spices, and Nuts and Seeds

Chiles: Clean chiles with damp paper towel, then arrange in air-fryer basket. Place basket into air fryer and set temperature to 350 degrees. Cook until fragrant and puffed, 1 to 3 minutes. Immediately remove from air fryer to stop toasting. Let chiles cool before stemming and seeding.

Whole Spices: Arrange whole spices in 6-inch round nonstick or silicone cake pan. Place pan in air-fryer basket and place basket into air fryer. Set temperature to 350 degrees. Cook, shaking basket occasionally, until spices are fragrant, 1 to 3 minutes. Immediately remove from pan.

Nuts and Seeds: Arrange nuts or seeds in 6-inch round nonstick or silicone cake pan. Place pan in air-fryer basket and place basket into air fryer. Set temperature to 350 degrees. Cook, shaking basket occasionally, until nuts or seeds are fragrant, 1 to 3 minutes. Immediately remove from pan.

Roast Garlic, Tomatoes, and Fruit

Roasted Garlic: Use this garlic in spreads, compound butter, and dips such as hummus.

Remove outer papery skins from 1 large head of garlic. Cut off top third of head to expose cloves and discard. Place garlic head, cut side up, in center of large piece of aluminum foil; drizzle with ½ teaspoon extra-virgin olive oil; and sprinkle with pinch table salt. Gather foil tightly around garlic to form packet and place packet in air-fryer basket. Place basket into air fryer; set temperature to 400 degrees; and cook until garlic is soft and golden, about 20 minutes. Carefully open packet to let garlic cool slightly. When cool enough to handle, squeeze cloves from skins; discard skins. Makes about 2 tablespoons; this recipe can be easily doubled; wrap garlic heads separately.

Roasted Plum Tomatoes: Use these tomatoes on a charcuterie board or as a sandwich topping, or serve them alongside roasted chicken, beef, pork, or fish.

Toss 1 pound plum tomatoes with 1 tablespoon extra-virgin olive oil, 2 thinly sliced garlic cloves, 1 teaspoon sugar, ¼ teaspoon dried oregano, ¼ teaspoon dried thyme, ¼ teaspoon table salt, and pinch red pepper flakes in bowl. Arrange tomatoes in even layer in air-fryer basket. Place basket into air fryer and set temperature to 350 degrees. Cook until tomatoes are shriveled, dry, and dark around edges, 20 to 30 minutes. Serve warm or at room temperature. (Tomatoes can be refrigerated for up to 3 days.) Makes about 1 cup; this recipe can be easily doubled (see page 10).

Roasted Fruit Topping: We had good success roasting apples, pears, peaches, plums, and pineapple in the air fryer. Add a pinch of cinnamon and/or 1 to 2 teaspoons of brown sugar, maple syrup, or honey (depending on the fruit's sweetness) before roasting. Stir in 1 to 2 tablespoons of toasted nuts, seeds, or shredded coconut before serving. Spoon topping over porridge or layer it with yogurt and granola.

Toss 3 cups 1-inch fruit pieces with oil and pinch table salt in 6-inch round nonstick or silicone cake pan. Place pan in air-fryer basket and place basket into air fryer. Set temperature to 400 degrees. Cook until fruit is tender and lightly browned, 15 to 20 minutes, stirring halfway through cooking. Serve warm or at room temperature. (Roasted fruit can be refrigerated for up to 3 days.) Makes about 1 cup; this recipe can be easily doubled in a 1½-quart soufflé dish (see page 10).

Bake Desserts
Apple Crisp
Serves 2 | Total Time: 1 hour

You will need a 3-cup ovensafe bowl for this recipe. Before starting, confirm your air fryer allows enough space for the dish. This recipe can be easily doubled; use a 1½-quart soufflé dish (see page 10) and bake for the same amount of time.

2 Golden Delicious apples, peeled, cored, and cut into ¾-inch pieces

5 teaspoons packed brown sugar, divided

2 teaspoons lemon juice

⅛ teaspoon plus pinch table salt, divided

⅛ teaspoon ground cinnamon

2 tablespoons all-purpose flour

1 tablespoon old-fashioned rolled oats

1 tablespoon unsalted butter

1 Toss apples with 2 teaspoons sugar, lemon juice, ⅛ teaspoon salt, and cinnamon in large bowl. Transfer to 3-cup ovensafe bowl and cover tightly with aluminum foil. Place bowl in air-fryer basket. Place basket into air fryer; set temperature to 400 degrees; and bake until apples are tender and begin to collapse, 30 to 35 minutes.

2 Meanwhile, mix flour, oats, remaining 1 tablespoon sugar, and remaining pinch salt together in second bowl. Using your fingers, rub butter into flour mixture until mixture has texture of coarse crumbs. Remove basket from air fryer. Discard foil and scatter topping evenly over apples. Return basket to air fryer and bake until topping is evenly browned and filling is just bubbling at edges, 5 to 7 minutes. Let crisp cool for 5 minutes before serving.

Per Serving Cal 210 | Total Fat 6g | Sat Fat 3.5g | Chol 15mg | Sodium 220mg Total Carb 39g | Dietary Fiber 5g | Total Sugars 26g | Added Sugars 7g | Protein 2g

Warm Chocolate Fudge Cakes
Serves 2 | Total Time: 35 minutes

You will need two 6-ounce ramekins for this recipe. This recipe can be easily doubled (see page 10).

3 ounces bittersweet chocolate, chopped

¼ cup milk

1 large egg

2 tablespoons canola oil

2 tablespoons packed brown sugar

¼ teaspoon vanilla extract

¼ teaspoon baking powder

⅛ teaspoon baking soda

⅛ teaspoon table salt

6 tablespoons (1¾ ounces) all-purpose flour

1 Microwave chocolate and milk in medium bowl at 50 percent power, stirring occasionally, until mixture is smooth, about 2 minutes. Whisk in egg, oil, sugar, vanilla, baking powder, baking soda, and salt. Gently whisk in flour until combined.

2 Grease two 6-ounce ramekins. Divide batter between prepared ramekins. Place ramekins in air-fryer basket, then place basket into air fryer. Set temperature to 325 degrees and bake until cakes have risen above rim of ramekins and tops are just firm to touch, 8 to 10 minutes. Let cool for 5 minutes before serving.

Per Serving Cal 340 | Total Fat 17g | Sat Fat 8g | Chol 95mg | Sodium 330mg Total Carb 42g | Dietary Fiber 2g | Total Sugars 8g | Added Sugars 7g | Protein 9g

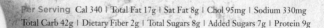

BREAKFAST

16 Egg in a Hole with Tomato, Avocado, and Herb Salad

19 Baked Eggs with Smoky Zucchini, Red Pepper, and Bread Hash

20 Baked Eggs with Spinach, Artichokes, and Feta

23 Kale, Roasted Red Pepper, and Goat Cheese Frittata
Ham, Pea, and Swiss Cheese Frittata
Broccoli, Sun-Dried Tomato, and Cheddar Frittata

24 Make-Ahead Breakfast Burritos

27 Hearty Vegetable Hash with Golden Yogurt

28 Roasted Fruit and Almond Butter Toast

31 Overnight Breakfast Grain Bowl
Overnight Breakfast Three-Grain Bowl

32 Make-Ahead Fruit, Nut, and Oat Scones
Currant, Almond, and Oat Scones with Earl Grey Glaze
Apricot, Pistachio, and Oat Scones with Garam Masala Glaze

35 Whole-Wheat Blueberry-Almond Muffins

EGG IN A HOLE WITH TOMATO, AVOCADO, AND HERB SALAD

Serves 1 | Total Time: 45 minutes

Why This Recipe Works For this skillet classic, you won't need a skillet nor have to stand at the stove to toast your bread and cook the egg. The air fryer's convection heat does both, leaving your hands free to make a lemony avocado, tomato, and herb salad. A flavorful olive oil–Dijon mustard mixture creates a barrier under the toasting bread, which prevents the egg white from leaking out. When the egg is nearly done, we turn off the air fryer and let the egg sit in the warm machine to finish setting the white without overcooking the yolk. If you don't have a round cutter, cut the toast hole with a sturdy drinking glass. Depending on the size of your air fryer, you may need to trim the bread slice to lay flat in the basket. This recipe can be easily doubled (see page 10).

Olive oil spray

1 teaspoon extra-virgin olive oil, plus extra for drizzling

1 teaspoon Dijon mustard

1 (½-inch-thick) slice rustic whole-grain bread

1 large egg

Pinch table salt

Pinch pepper

2 ounces cherry tomatoes, halved

½ avocado, cut into ½-inch pieces

⅓ cup torn fresh parsley leaves

1 scallion, sliced thin

2 teaspoons lemon juice

1 Line bottom of air-fryer basket with aluminum foil and lightly spray foil with oil spray.

2 Whisk oil and mustard together in medium bowl. Using 2-inch round cutter, cut and remove circle from center of bread. Brush both sides of bread slice and cut-out with oil mixture; do not clean bowl. Arrange bread slice and cutout in prepared basket. Place basket into air fryer; set temperature to 400 degrees; and cook until bread is heated through but still soft, about 4 minutes, flipping bread halfway through cooking.

3 Working quickly, crack egg into bread hole, lightly spray with oil spray, and sprinkle with salt and pepper. Return basket to air fryer and cook until egg white is opaque but still slightly jiggly, 4 to 6 minutes. Turn off air fryer and let bread sit, without moving, until egg white is set, 2 to 4 minutes.

4 Meanwhile, toss tomatoes, avocado, parsley, scallion, and lemon juice together in now-empty bowl. Season with salt and pepper to taste. Using spatula, transfer bread slice and cutout to plate. Top with salad and drizzle with extra oil. Serve.

Per Serving Cal 450 | Total Fat 27g | Sat Fat 5g | Chol 185mg | Sodium 580mg
Total Carb 39g | Dietary Fiber 9g | Total Sugars 7g | Added Sugars 0g | Protein 17g

BAKED EGGS WITH SMOKY ZUCCHINI, RED PEPPER, AND BREAD HASH

Serves 1 | Total Time: 45 minutes (30 minutes from refrigerated)

Why This Recipe Works We know that the air fryer is hands-off and turns out perfectly cooked eggs with creamy, slightly runny yolks and tender whites. But we wanted something more to sink our teeth into. Instead of making potato hash, we added healthful zucchini, roasted red peppers, and whole-grain bread, flavored with red wine vinegar and smoked paprika, to our eggs. The hash created insulation between the eggs and the very hot sides of the ovensafe bowl, preventing the eggs from cooking too quickly. Turning off the air fryer when the egg whites had just turned opaque but still jiggled and letting the eggs sit for 6 minutes in the warm machine completed the cooking. The residual heat set the whites without overcooking the yolks. You will need a 3-cup ovensafe bowl for this recipe; before starting this recipe, confirm your air fryer allows enough space for the dish. This recipe can be easily doubled in a 1½-quart soufflé dish (see page 10); make four indentations in step 3.

½ zucchini (4 ounces), cut into ½-inch pieces

¼ cup jarred roasted red peppers, rinsed, patted dry, and chopped

1 slice rustic whole-grain bread, cut into ½-inch pieces (1 cup)

1 tablespoon tomato paste

2 teaspoons extra-virgin olive oil, plus extra for drizzling

1 teaspoon red wine vinegar

1 teaspoon smoked paprika

2 large eggs

Olive oil spray

Pinch table salt

1 tablespoon chopped fresh parsley

1 Combine zucchini, peppers, bread, tomato paste, oil, vinegar, and paprika in 3-cup ovensafe bowl. (Vegetable-bread mixture can be covered and refrigerated for up to 24 hours.)

2 Place bowl in air-fryer basket. Place basket into air fryer; set temperature to 400 degrees; and cook until zucchini is tender and edges of bread begin to brown, 8 to 10 minutes, stirring halfway through cooking.

3 Remove basket from air fryer and reduce temperature to 250 degrees. Make two shallow 2-inch-wide indentations in vegetable-bread mixture using back of spoon. Crack 1 egg into each indentation, lightly spray with oil spray, and sprinkle with salt.

4 Return basket to air fryer and cook until egg whites are opaque but still slightly jiggly, 6 to 8 minutes. Turn off air fryer and let eggs sit, without moving, until whites are set, 6 to 8 minutes. Sprinkle eggs with parsley and drizzle with extra oil. Serve.

Per Serving Cal 430 | Total Fat 22g | Sat Fat 5g | Chol 370mg | Sodium 810mg
Total Carb 36g | Dietary Fiber 2g | Total Sugars 11g | Added Sugars 0g | Protein 23g

BAKED EGGS WITH SPINACH, ARTICHOKES, AND FETA

Serves 1 | Total Time: 45 minutes (30 minutes from refrigerated)

Why This Recipe Works These easy air-fryer baked eggs are packed with meaty artichokes, spinach, and tangy feta, which give you oodles of flavor. They're also fuss-free. The vegetables can be prepped the night before, so this dish is perfect for a weekday breakfast. And you eat them out of the bowl you use to air-fry them. The air fryer's dry heat cooks refrigerated or frozen vegetables quickly, reducing prep, cook, and cleanup time. Creating two indentations in the spinach mixture separates the eggs slightly, helping them cook through, warmed by the vegetables, better than if they were nestled together, with whites touching. Lemon juice and dill cut the eggs' richness. We prefer the flavor and texture of jarred whole baby artichokes but you can substitute 3 ounces frozen artichokes, thawed, patted dry, and chopped coarse. You will need a 3-cup ovensafe bowl for this recipe; before starting this recipe, confirm your air fryer allows enough space for the dish. This recipe can be easily doubled in a 1½-quart soufflé dish (see page 10); make four indentations in step 2.

5 ounces frozen chopped spinach, thawed and squeezed dry	1 tablespoon minced fresh dill, divided	2 large eggs
		Olive oil spray
½ cup jarred whole baby artichokes, patted dry and chopped coarse	2 teaspoons extra-virgin olive oil, plus extra for drizzling	Pinch table salt
	1 teaspoon lemon juice	2 tablespoons crumbled feta cheese
1 scallion, sliced thin	Pinch ground nutmeg	

1 Combine spinach, artichokes, scallion, 2 teaspoons dill, oil, lemon juice, and nutmeg in 3-cup ovensafe bowl, then spread into even layer. (Spinach mixture can be covered and refrigerated for up to 24 hours.)

2 Make two shallow 2-inch-wide indentations in spinach mixture using back of spoon, then place bowl in air-fryer basket. Place basket into air fryer; set temperature to 400 degrees; and cook until edges of spinach mixture begin to brown, about 8 minutes.

3 Remove basket from air fryer and reduce temperature to 250 degrees. Crack 1 egg into each indentation, lightly spray with oil spray, and sprinkle with salt. Return basket to air fryer and cook until egg whites are opaque but still slightly jiggly, 6 to 8 minutes.

4 Turn off air fryer and let eggs sit, without moving, until whites are set, 6 to 8 minutes. Sprinkle eggs and spinach mixture with feta and remaining 1 teaspoon dill and drizzle with extra oil. Serve.

Per Serving Cal 340 | Total Fat 23g | Sat Fat 7g | Chol 385mg | Sodium 740mg
Total Carb 14g | Dietary Fiber 6g | Total Sugars 3g | Added Sugars 0g | Protein 22g

KALE, ROASTED RED PEPPER, AND GOAT CHEESE FRITTATA

Serves 2 | Total Time: 30 minutes

Why This Recipe Works This frittata highlights the incredible convenience and even cooking offered by the air fryer. In about fifteen minutes (plus the time it takes to combine a few ingredients in a bowl), it transformed a simple egg-and-cheese custard packed with kale, roasted red peppers, and scallions into a delightful meal for two—fluffy and tender on the inside, golden and delicately sealed on the outside. The compact size and even heat of a nonstick cake pan made the occasional stirring of the egg mixture during cooking unnecessary. Using frozen vegetables (which are blanched before freezing) meant we didn't have to precook them. Any worries we had that frozen vegetables might taste soggy were put to rest by the air fryer's rapidly circulating hot air, which gently roasted the vegetables at the surface and edges of the frittata. You will need a 6-inch round nonstick or silicone cake pan for this recipe; before starting this recipe, confirm your air fryer allows enough space for the pan.

4 large eggs

1 tablespoon milk

⅛ teaspoon table salt

4 ounces frozen chopped kale or spinach, thawed and squeezed dry

¼ cup jarred roasted red peppers, rinsed, patted dry, and chopped

1 ounce goat cheese, crumbled (¼ cup)

2 scallions, sliced thin

1 Generously spray 6-inch round nonstick cake pan with canola oil spray. Whisk eggs, milk, and salt in medium bowl until well combined, then stir in kale, peppers, goat cheese, and scallions.

2 Transfer egg mixture to prepared pan and place pan in air-fryer basket. Place basket into air fryer; set temperature to 350 degrees; and cook until frittata is deep golden brown and registers 180 to 190 degrees, 15 to 25 minutes.

3 Transfer pan to wire rack and let rest for 5 minutes. Using rubber spatula, loosen frittata from pan and transfer to cutting board. Cut into wedges and serve.

HAM, PEA, AND SWISS CHEESE FRITTATA

Substitute 2 ounces chopped deli ham and ½ cup thawed frozen peas for kale and red peppers, and Swiss cheese for goat cheese.

BROCCOLI, SUN-DRIED TOMATO, AND CHEDDAR FRITTATA

Substitute 4 ounces frozen chopped broccoli florets, thawed and patted dry, and 2 tablespoons chopped oil-packed sun-dried tomatoes, rinsed and patted dry, for kale and red peppers, and cheddar cheese for goat cheese.

Per Serving Cal 210 | Total Fat 13g | Sat Fat 5g | Chol 380mg | Sodium 450mg
Total Carb 6g | Dietary Fiber 2g | Total Sugars 2g | Added Sugars 0g | Protein 17g

MAKE-AHEAD BREAKFAST BURRITOS

Makes 6 burritos | **Total Time: 45 minutes**

Why This Recipe Works If you love a good breakfast burrito and want one quickly, this recipe is for you. Though the filling is made in a skillet, shaped burritos can be warmed in the air fryer from refrigerated or frozen. Unlike the microwave, the air fryer heats evenly, so there are no soggy or cold bits. While store-bought breakfast burritos often rely on greasy meat for bulk and flavor, we fill our burrito with more nutritious refried black beans and added frozen chopped kale to our fluffy scrambled eggs. To build a flavorful base for the beans, we sautéed aromatic scallions, cumin, and chili powder. We added our beans, mashing them while they cooked, to create a cohesive mixture. To freeze the burritos, wrap each one in foil. The number of burritos you can cook at one time will depend on the size of your air fryer. Serve with salsa, Greek yogurt, lime wedges, and hot sauce.

- 8 large eggs
- ¼ cup milk
- ⅛ teaspoon table salt
- 2 tablespoons extra-virgin olive oil, divided
- 8 ounces frozen chopped kale or spinach, thawed and squeezed dry

- 6 scallions, sliced thin
- 1½ teaspoons ground cumin
- ½ teaspoon chili powder
- 1 (15-ounce) can black beans

- ¼ cup chopped fresh cilantro
- 2 tablespoons lime juice
- 6 (10-inch) 100 percent whole-wheat tortillas

1 Whisk eggs, milk, and salt in large bowl until well combined. Heat 1 tablespoon oil in 12-inch nonstick skillet over medium heat until shimmering. Add egg mixture and, using rubber spatula, constantly and firmly scrape along bottom and sides of skillet until eggs are just set, 2 to 4 minutes. Off heat, fold in kale. Transfer egg mixture to plate and wipe skillet clean with paper towels.

2 Heat remaining 1 tablespoon oil in now-empty skillet over medium heat until shimmering. Add scallions, cumin, and chili powder and cook until fragrant, about 1 minute. Stir in beans and their canning liquid and cook, mashing beans with back of spoon, until mixture is heated through and thickened, 3 to 5 minutes. Off heat, stir in cilantro and lime juice. Season with salt and pepper to taste.

3 Wrap tortillas in damp dish towel and microwave until warm and pliable, about 1 minute. Lay tortillas on counter and spread bean mixture evenly across each tortilla, close to bottom edge. Top with egg-kale mixture. Working with 1 tortilla at a time, fold sides, then bottom of tortilla over filling, then continue to roll tightly into wrap.

4 Arrange up to 4 burritos, seam side down, in air-fryer basket, spaced evenly apart. Place basket into air fryer; set temperature to 400 degrees; and cook until crisp, 5 to 8 minutes.

5 Individually wrap remaining burritos in greased aluminum foil. Transfer to zipper-lock bags and freeze for up to 2 months. To bake from frozen, place foil-wrapped burritos into air-fryer basket. Place basket into air fryer; set temperature to 325 degrees; and cook until heated through, about 30 minutes, flipping burritos halfway through cooking. Let rest, wrapped in foil, for 5 minutes before serving. (Alternatively, frozen wrapped burritos can be thawed in refrigerator overnight and baked for about 15 minutes.)

Per Serving Cal 420 | Total Fat 16g | Sat Fat 4g | Chol 250mg | Sodium 940mg
Total Carb 45g | Dietary Fiber 4g | Total Sugars 2g | Added Sugars 0g | Protein 21g

HEARTY VEGETABLE HASH WITH GOLDEN YOGURT

Serves 2 | Total Time: 35 minutes

Why This Recipe Works Magic happens when you cook vegetables in an air fryer. In minutes, you have the crisped exteriors, tender interiors, and caramelized deliciousness you usually associate with oven roasting. We transformed that roasted veggie concept into a quick, flavorful hash you can eat for a healthy breakfast (or lunch or dinner). We used nutrient-dense sweet potatoes and meaty mushrooms along with shallots, which crisped up nicely in the air fryer. To start our day with some fresh greens, we also incorporated raw baby kale. We tried air frying the kale with the other vegetables, but it burnt long before the sweet potatoes and mushrooms were done. Instead, we tossed the warm vegetables with the kale to wilt it. We drizzled a silky-smooth yogurt sauce, flavored with cumin, turmeric, and cilantro, over the hash. A sprinkling of pistachios added some protein and a finishing crunch. This recipe can be easily doubled (see page 10); increase cooking time to about 45 minutes, stirring twice during cooking. For more information on toasting nuts in the air fryer, see page 12.

- 4 teaspoons extra-virgin olive oil, divided
- ¼ teaspoon ground cumin
- ¼ teaspoon ground turmeric
- ¼ cup plain yogurt
- 1 tablespoon minced fresh cilantro

- ½ teaspoon table salt, divided
- 1 pound sweet potatoes, peeled and cut into ½-inch pieces
- 12 ounces cremini mushrooms, trimmed and quartered
- 2 shallots, sliced thin

- ¼ teaspoon pepper
- 2 ounces (2 cups) baby kale
- ¼ cup shelled pistachios, toasted and chopped

1 Combine 1 teaspoon oil, cumin, and turmeric in small bowl and microwave until fragrant, about 1 minute. Stir in yogurt, cilantro, and ¼ teaspoon salt; set aside for serving.

2 Toss potatoes, mushrooms, and shallots with pepper, remaining 1 tablespoon oil, and remaining ¼ teaspoon salt in large bowl; transfer to air-fryer basket. Place basket into air fryer and set temperature to 400 degrees. Cook until vegetables are tender and golden brown, 18 to 20 minutes, stirring halfway through cooking.

3 Return vegetables to now-empty bowl. Add kale and toss gently to combine. Drizzle individual portions with yogurt sauce and sprinkle with pistachios before serving.

Per Serving Cal 400 | Total Fat 18g | Sat Fat 3g | Chol 5mg | Sodium 720mg
Total Carb 52g | Dietary Fiber 10g | Total Sugars 15g | Added Sugars 0g | Protein 13g

ROASTED FRUIT AND ALMOND BUTTER TOAST

Serves 1 | Total Time: 15 minutes

Why This Recipe Works Why make toast in an air fryer? Because turning on that one appliance quickly gives you not only toasty bread but also melted almond or peanut butter and roasted fruit all in a single step. While developing this recipe, we weren't sure if we would have to pretoast the bread, take it out, top it with fruit, and put it back in the air fryer. But we found that the air fryer's rapidly circulating heat perfectly toasted the bread and caramelized the fruit all at once in less than 10 minutes. To save even more time, rather than tossing the uncooked fruit in sugar before laying it on the bread, we sweetened it afterward, drizzling the toast with a little honey or maple syrup. We preferred bananas, grapes, and berries here; citrus tends to dry up and turn bitter in the air fryer. Depending on the size of your air fryer, you may need to trim the bread slice to lay flat in the basket. Let your creativity run wild with the fruit you use; use a single variety or a combination. Customize your toast with additional toppings such as toasted nuts, seeds, or shredded coconut. This recipe can be easily doubled (see page 10).

2 ounces ripe banana, seedless grapes, blueberries, raspberries, and/or hulled strawberries

2 tablespoons natural, unsweetened almond or peanut butter

1 (½-inch-thick) slice rustic whole-grain bread

½ teaspoon honey or maple syrup

Slice banana ¼ inch thick, halve grapes, and/or quarter strawberries. Spread almond butter onto bread and top evenly with fruit. Place bread into air-fryer basket. Place basket into air fryer and set temperature to 400 degrees.

Cook until fruit begins to caramelize and toast is golden brown around edges, 6 to 10 minutes. Transfer bread to plate and drizzle with honey. Serve.

Per Serving Cal 390 | Total Fat 20g | Sat Fat 2.5g | Chol 0mg | Sodium 290mg
Total Carb 42g | Dietary Fiber 4g | Total Sugars 13g | Added Sugars 3g | Protein 15g

OVERNIGHT BREAKFAST GRAIN BOWL

Serves 1 | Total Time: 1 hour, plus 8 hours soaking

Why This Recipe Works We love whole grains for a healthy breakfast but they take a lot of attention to prepare. Could we use the air fryer's even temperature for hands-off cooking? We chose quinoa for this porridge and found that presoaking and cooking the grains in plenty of liquid encouraged them to swell, burst, and release their starches, creating creaminess. We air-fried the soaked grains and, in 45 minutes, our porridge was ready without boiling over or needing constant stirring. Maple syrup and berries are an appetizing topping, and a splash of fruity olive oil is a flavorful, healthy change from butter. For savory porridge, skip the syrup and fruit and mix in your favorite cheese and fresh herbs. For an accurate measurement of boiling water, bring a kettle of water to a boil and then measure out the desired amount. This recipe can be easily doubled using a 1½-quart soufflé dish (see page 10). You will need a 3-cup ovensafe bowl for this recipe; before starting this recipe, confirm your air fryer allows enough space for the dish. Customize your porridge with additional toppings such as yogurt, toasted nuts and seeds, and/or our Roasted Fruit Topping (page 12).

5 tablespoons prewashed white quinoa	⅛ teaspoon table salt	1½ teaspoons maple syrup, plus extra for drizzling
1¼ cups boiling water	2-4 tablespoons milk	
⅛ teaspoon ground cinnamon	1 tablespoon extra-virgin olive oil	¼ cup blackberries, blueberries, and/or raspberries

1 Add quinoa to 3-cup ovensafe bowl. Cover with cold water and soak at room temperature for at least 8 hours or up to 24 hours. Drain and rinse well.

2 Combine quinoa, boiling water, cinnamon, and salt in now-empty bowl and cover tightly with aluminum foil. Place bowl in air-fryer basket. Place basket into air fryer; set temperature to 400 degrees; and cook until quinoa is tender and beginning to burst, about 45 minutes.

3 Remove basket from air fryer. Stir 2 tablespoons milk, oil, and maple syrup into porridge and let sit, uncovered, for 5 minutes; porridge will thicken as it sits. Adjust consistency with remaining 2 tablespoons milk as needed. Top with berries and drizzle with extra maple syrup before serving.

OVERNIGHT BREAKFAST THREE-GRAIN BOWL
Reduce quinoa to 2 tablespoons. Soak 2 tablespoons millet and 1 tablespoon amaranth with quinoa in step 1.

Per Serving Cal 480 | Total Fat 18g | Sat Fat 2.5g | Chol 0mg | Sodium 310mg
Total Carb 73g | Dietary Fiber 9g | Total Sugars 30g | Added Sugars 6g | Protein 10g

MAKE-AHEAD FRUIT, NUT, AND OAT SCONES

Makes 10 | Total Time: 45 minutes (25 minutes from frozen)

Why This Recipe Works Who wouldn't want a healthy breakfast scone that can be made ahead of time? Our scones can be easily baked in the air fryer, even directly from frozen. We toasted both oats and nuts in the air fryer to enhance their flavor, and since dried fruits are naturally concentrated in sweetness, we could cut back on sugar. Our biggest challenge was temperature. At 400 degrees, the exterior became too dark before the scone baked all the way through. But dropping the temperature to 350 meant the exterior and interior finished cooking at the same time. We developed this recipe with raisins and walnuts, but any dried fruit and nuts will work. The number of scones you can cook at one time will depend on the size of your air fryer. For the variations, extra glaze can be stored in an airtight container for up to a week. For more information on toasting nuts in the air fryer, see page 12.

½ cup whole milk

1 large egg

1½ cups (7½ ounces) all-purpose flour

¼ cup (1¾ ounces) plus 1 tablespoon sugar, divided

2 teaspoons baking powder

½ teaspoon table salt

8 tablespoons unsalted butter, chilled, cut into ½-inch pieces

1¼ cups (3¾ ounces) old-fashioned rolled oats, toasted

½ cup raisins

¼ cup walnuts, toasted and chopped

1 Whisk milk and egg together in bowl; measure out and reserve 1 tablespoon milk mixture. Pulse flour, ¼ cup sugar, baking powder, and salt in food processor until combined, about 4 pulses. Scatter butter over top and pulse until mixture resembles coarse cornmeal, 12 to 14 pulses. Transfer mixture to large bowl and stir in oats, raisins, and walnuts. Stir in remaining milk mixture until large clumps form. Continue to mix dough by hand in bowl until dough forms cohesive mass.

2 Turn dough and any floury bits onto lightly floured counter; pat gently into 7-inch circle. Cut dough into 10 wedges. Brush tops with reserved 1 tablespoon milk mixture and sprinkle with remaining 1 tablespoon sugar.

3 Lightly spray base of air-fryer basket with canola oil spray. Space desired number of scones at least ½ inch apart in prepared basket; evenly space remaining scones on parchment paper–lined rimmed baking sheet. Place basket into air fryer and set temperature to 350 degrees. Bake until scones are golden brown, 10 to 15 minutes. Transfer scones to wire rack and let cool for at least 5 minutes before serving.

4 Freeze remaining sheet of scones until firm, about 1 hour. Transfer scones to 1-gallon zipper-lock bag and freeze for up to 1 month. To bake from frozen, place scones into air-fryer basket. Place basket into air fryer, set temperature to 250 degrees, and bake for 10 minutes. Increase temperature to 350 degrees and continue to bake until golden brown, about 10 minutes.

CURRANT, ALMOND, AND OAT SCONES WITH EARL GREY GLAZE

Substitute currants for raisins and almonds for walnuts. Microwave 1 tablespoon milk and ½ teaspoon crumbled Earl Grey tea leaves in medium bowl until steaming, about 30 seconds. Let cool completely, about 10 minutes. Whisk in ½ cup confectioners' sugar until smooth and let sit until thick but pourable, about 10 minutes. Omit sugar for sprinkling. Let scones cool to room temperature, about 20 minutes, then drizzle with glaze. Let glaze set for 10 minutes before serving.

APRICOT, PISTACHIO, AND OAT SCONES WITH GARAM MASALA GLAZE

Substitute chopped dried apricots for raisins and pistachios for walnuts. Microwave 1 tablespoon milk and ½ teaspoon garam masala in medium bowl until steaming, about 30 seconds. Let cool completely, about 10 minutes. Whisk in ½ cup confectioners' sugar until smooth and let sit until thick but pourable, about 10 minutes. Omit sugar for sprinkling. Let scones cool to room temperature, about 20 minutes, then drizzle with glaze. Let glaze set for 10 minutes before serving.

Per Serving Cal 320 | Total Fat 12g | Sat Fat 6g | Chol 45mg | Sodium 230mg
Total Carb 30g | Dietary Fiber 1g | Total Sugars 24g | Added Sugars 6g | Protein 5g

WHOLE-WHEAT BLUEBERRY-ALMOND MUFFINS

Makes 4 muffins | Total Time: 45 minutes

Why This Recipe Works We wanted to build a healthy whole-wheat blueberry muffin (scaled to make four quick, one-bowl muffins) that would be a breeze to bake in the air fryer. The problem is, most whole-wheat muffins are dense and heavy. Could we create an air-fried version that was tender and delicious? First, we addressed the cardboard-like flavor of many whole-wheat muffins. We replaced part of the whole-wheat flour with finely chopped almonds and loved how their rich nuttiness complemented the wheat's own earthy, toasty flavor. But the muffins were still squat and dense. We tried combining two leaveners—baking soda and baking powder—and were surprised to find the muffins became too tender, lacking the structure to even come out of the muffin tins. Incorporating just a little all-purpose flour into the mix brought structural integrity and tenderness to our muffins.

3 tablespoons sugar

¾ teaspoon baking powder

⅛ teaspoon baking soda

¼ teaspoon table salt

¼ teaspoon ground cinnamon

⅓ cup plain yogurt

1 large egg

2 tablespoons canola oil

½ teaspoon vanilla extract

⅓ cup (1¾ ounces) whole-wheat flour

¼ cup (1¼ ounces) all-purpose flour

¼ cup finely chopped almonds, divided

⅓ cup fresh or frozen blueberries

1 Spray 4 aluminum foil or silicone muffin-tin liners with canola oil spray. Whisk sugar, baking powder, baking soda, salt, and cinnamon together in medium bowl. Whisk in yogurt, egg, oil, and vanilla until smooth. Using rubber spatula, stir whole-wheat flour, all-purpose flour, and 2 tablespoons almonds into yogurt mixture until just combined (do not overmix). Fold in blueberries gently until incorporated.

2 Divide batter evenly among prepared muffin-tin liners (liners will be filled to rim) and sprinkle with remaining almonds. Place muffin-tin liners in air-fryer basket. Place basket into air fryer; set temperature to 350 degrees; and bake until muffins are golden brown and toothpick inserted in center comes out with few crumbs attached, 12 to 14 minutes.

3 Transfer muffins to wire rack and let cool for at least 10 minutes before serving.

Per Serving Cal 240 | Total Fat 12g | Sat Fat 1.5g | Chol 50mg | Sodium 290mg
Total Carb 29g | Dietary Fiber 2g | Total Sugars 12g | Added Sugars 9g | Protein 6g

POULTRY

38 Turkey-Zucchini Meatballs with Orzo, Spiced Tomato Sauce, and Feta

41 California Turkey Burgers

42 Crispy Breaded Chicken Breasts with Creamy Apple-Fennel Salad

45 Prosciutto-Wrapped Chicken with Cantaloupe-Cucumber Salad

46 Brown Sugar–Balsamic-Glazed Bone-In Chicken Breast
Peach-Jalapeño-Glazed Bone-In Chicken Breast
Honey-Miso-Glazed Bone-In Chicken Breast

48 Spicy Peanut Chicken with Charred Green Beans and Tomatoes

50 Chipotle-Honey Fried Chicken with Brussels Sprout and Citrus Salad

52 Roasted Chicken Thighs with Potatoes and Mesclun Salad

55 Chicken Thighs with Roasted Mushrooms and Tomatoes

56 Coriander Chicken Thighs with Roasted Cauliflower and Shallots

58 Spiced Chicken Kebabs with Vegetable and Bulgur Salad

61 Chicken and Chickpea Salad with Carrots, Cucumbers, and Feta

62 Hoisin-Ginger Chicken Salad with Napa Cabbage, Shiitakes, and Bell Pepper

64 Chicken-Tomatillo Tacos with Roasted Pineapple Salsa

67 Roasted Chicken Sausages with Butternut Squash and Radicchio

68 Whole Roast Chicken with Lemon, Dill, and Garlic
with Orange, Aleppo, and Cinnamon
with Ginger, Cumin, and Cardamom

TURKEY-ZUCCHINI MEATBALLS WITH ORZO, SPICED TOMATO SAUCE, AND FETA

Serves 2 | Total Time: 1 hour

Why This Recipe Works Cooking pasta or grains in the air fryer can be tricky since the environment encourages rapid evaporation, which can lead to uneven cooking. Enter orzo—a rice-shaped pasta with a rare talent for maintaining its shape and texture when cooked, especially when pretoasted. So we pretoasted the orzo in olive oil and garlic, using a 6-inch cake pan. Then we parcooked the pasta in a warmly spiced tomato sauce. Meanwhile, we shaped our turkey meatballs using shredded zucchini, a healthy way to add vegetables to the dish, replace the traditional panade, and give the meatballs moisture and tenderness. We nestled the meatballs into the parcooked orzo and sauce, then air-fried the meatballs until they had simmered on the bottom and were lightly roasted on the top. Finally, we added crumbled feta and air-fried everything together for the last few minutes. By the time the meatballs had reached their proper temperature, the cheese had melted and was just beginning to brown. You can substitute traditional orzo for the whole-wheat orzo; do not substitute other pasta shapes. Be sure to use ground turkey, not ground turkey breast (also labeled 99 percent fat-free), in this recipe. Ground chicken also works well here. You will need a 6-inch round nonstick or silicone cake pan for this recipe; before starting this recipe, confirm your air fryer allows enough space for the pan.

½ cup 100 percent whole-wheat orzo

1 tablespoon extra-virgin olive oil, plus extra for drizzling

2 garlic cloves, minced, divided

1 (8-ounce) can tomato sauce

¾ cup water

¼ teaspoon pepper, divided

⅛ teaspoon ground cinnamon

Pinch ground cloves

8 ounces ground turkey

4 ounces zucchini, grated (¾ cup)

1 tablespoon minced fresh oregano, plus extra for serving

⅛ teaspoon table salt

1 ounce crumbled feta cheese (¼ cup)

1 Combine orzo, oil, and half of garlic in 6-inch round nonstick cake pan, then spread into even layer. Place pan into air-fryer basket and place basket into air fryer. Set temperature to 400 degrees and cook until orzo is lightly browned and fragrant, 3 to 5 minutes, stirring halfway through cooking.

2 Stir tomato sauce, water, ⅛ teaspoon pepper, cinnamon, and cloves into orzo mixture until evenly combined. Return basket to air fryer and cook until orzo is al dente, 18 to 22 minutes.

3 Using hands, lightly knead turkey, zucchini, oregano, salt, remaining garlic, and remaining ⅛ teaspoon pepper in medium bowl until mixture forms cohesive mass. Using lightly moistened hands, pinch off and roll mixture into 8 meatballs. (Meatballs can be refrigerated for up to 24 hours.)

4 Stir orzo mixture gently to recombine. Nestle meatballs into orzo and cook until meatballs are lightly browned, 8 to 10 minutes. Sprinkle feta over meatballs and cook until meatballs register 160 degrees and feta is spotty brown, 2 to 4 minutes.

5 Transfer pan to wire rack and let meatballs and orzo rest for 5 minutes. Drizzle with extra oil and sprinkle with extra oregano before serving.

Per Serving Cal 410 | Total Fat 13g | Sat Fat 5g | Chol 60mg | Sodium 880mg
Total Carb 40g | Dietary Fiber 2g | Total Sugars 7g | Added Sugars 0g | Protein 37g

CALIFORNIA TURKEY BURGERS

Serves 2 | Total Time: 45 minutes

Why This Recipe Works The air fryer seemed like a convenient way to make turkey burgers, but it wasn't as simple as forming two ground turkey patties and tossing them in the basket. On its own, ground turkey cooks up dry and dense—the extra-lean meat can't hold on to its own moisture during cooking. But we found that mixing in yogurt and panko gave the burgers structure and kept them moist. Making a slight indentation in the raw patties prevented them from puffing up too much as they cooked. And what's a California turkey burger without avocado? We decided to give the fruit a bit of a twist by pickling it, which added vibrancy and zip to the creamy avocado. Be sure to use ground turkey, not ground turkey breast (also labeled 99 percent fat-free), in this recipe. Ground chicken also works well here. This recipe can be easily doubled (see page 10).

½ avocado

1 small shallot, minced

1 teaspoon distilled white vinegar

¼ teaspoon sugar

¼ teaspoon table salt, divided

3 tablespoons plain yogurt

2 tablespoons panko bread crumbs

¼ teaspoon pepper

8 ounces ground turkey

2 slices Swiss, provolone, or pepper Jack cheese

2 hamburger buns, toasted if desired

½ tomato, sliced thin

1 ounce (½ cup) alfalfa sprouts

1 Using fork, mash avocado, shallot, vinegar, sugar, and ⅛ teaspoon salt to coarse paste in bowl; set aside for serving.

2 Lightly spray bottom of air-fryer basket with canola oil spray. Using fork, mash yogurt, panko, pepper, and remaining ⅛ teaspoon salt to paste in medium bowl. Add turkey and lightly knead with hands until mixture forms cohesive mass. Using lightly moistened hands, divide turkey mixture into 2 lightly packed balls, then flatten each gently into ½-inch-thick patty. Press center of each patty with your fingertips to create ¼-inch-deep depression.

3 Arrange patties in prepared basket, spaced evenly apart. Place basket into air fryer and set temperature to 350 degrees. Cook until burgers are lightly browned and register 160 degrees, 10 to 15 minutes, flipping halfway through cooking.

4 Turn off air fryer. Top burgers with cheese and let sit in warm air fryer until melted, about 1 minute. If desired, arrange bun tops and bottoms cut side up in now-empty basket. Return basket to air fryer, set temperature to 400, and cook until buns are lightly toasted, 4 to 6 minutes. Serve burgers on buns, topped with avocado mixture, tomato, and alfalfa sprouts.

Per Serving Cal 460 | Total Fat 19g | Sat Fat 8g | Chol 70mg | Sodium 710mg
Total Carb 36g | Dietary Fiber 4g | Total Sugars 8g | Added Sugars 1g | Protein 42g

CRISPY BREADED CHICKEN BREASTS WITH CREAMY APPLE-FENNEL SALAD

Serves 2 | Total Time: 45 minutes

Why This Recipe Works The convection heat of the air fryer quickly produced delectable golden-brown, breaded chicken breasts that crisped up with very little oil, tasting rich but staying low in calories. We also made an aromatic salad to accompany the dish, dressed with yogurt instead of mayonnaise. For the chicken, we found that panko worked better than ordinary bread crumbs for a crisp coating. The challenge was that the panko browned unevenly in the air fryer. Pretoasting the panko bread crumbs in the microwave with a little olive oil helped, guaranteeing evenly golden crusts. We also pounded the chicken breasts to facilitate even cooking and browning. To streamline the breading process, we whisked flour into an egg, added a generous dollop of Dijon mustard for brightness and tang, and quickly dipped the chicken into this mixture before dredging it with the toasted panko. For our salad, we whisked together a creamy rémoulade-style dressing of yogurt, Dijon mustard, caper brine, and lemon juice, tossing it with a thinly sliced fennel bulb, chopped apple, and capers. If your fennel does not have fronds, substitute 1 tablespoon fresh chopped dill or parsley. This recipe can be easily doubled (see page 10).

- 1 cup panko bread crumbs
- 2 tablespoons extra-virgin olive oil
- 1 large egg
- 4 teaspoons Dijon mustard, divided
- 1 tablespoon all-purpose flour

- ¼ teaspoon table salt
- 2 (6-ounce) boneless, skinless chicken breasts, trimmed
- 1 tablespoon plain yogurt
- 1 teaspoon lemon juice

- 1 teaspoon capers, rinsed, plus 1 teaspoon brine
- 1 fennel bulb, 1 tablespoon fronds minced, stalks discarded, bulb halved, cored, and sliced thin
- 1 apple, cored and cut into 2-inch-long matchsticks

1 Toss panko with oil in shallow dish until evenly coated. Microwave, stirring frequently, until light golden brown, 1 to 3 minutes; let cool slightly. Whisk egg, 1 tablespoon mustard, flour, and salt together in second shallow dish.

2 Pound chicken between 2 sheets of plastic wrap to uniform thickness. Pat dry with paper towels. Working with 1 breast at a time, dredge in egg mixture, letting excess drip off, then coat with panko, pressing gently to adhere.

3 Lightly spray bottom of air-fryer basket with canola oil spray. Arrange breasts in prepared basket, spaced evenly apart, alternating ends. Place basket into air fryer and set temperature to 400 degrees. Cook until chicken is crisp and registers 160 degrees, 12 to 18 minutes, flipping and rotating breasts halfway through cooking.

4 Whisk yogurt, lemon juice, caper brine, fennel fronds, and remaining 1 teaspoon mustard together in large bowl. Add apple, fennel bulb, and capers and toss to combine. Season with salt and pepper to taste. Serve chicken with salad.

Per Serving Cal 540 | Total Fat 17g | Sat Fat 3.5g | Chol 195mg | Sodium 740mg
Total Carb 46g | Dietary Fiber 6g | Total Sugars 15g | Added Sugars 0g | Protein 46g

PROSCIUTTO-WRAPPED CHICKEN WITH CANTALOUPE-CUCUMBER SALAD

Serves 2 | Total Time: 35 minutes

Why This Recipe Works Boneless, skinless chicken breasts are a great protein for healthy eating, but their leanness means they need to be kept moist during air frying. To do so, we wrapped each breast in two slices of salty prosciutto, the only seasoning and fat they needed. For a healthy plate, we added salad, using cantaloupe since prosciutto and cantaloupe are a classic pairing. We pounded the chicken breasts to a uniform thickness so that they would take the same time to air-fry and would cook through by the time the prosciutto fat rendered and the wrapper was crisp. The edges of the chicken also crisped up, adding pleasant crunch to the dish. Making the salad first allowed the cantaloupe and cucumber to absorb the flavorful dressing while the chicken cooked. Packaged, presliced prosciutto tends to yield more consistent slices than prosciutto from the deli counter. This recipe can be easily doubled (see page 10).

- 2 tablespoons extra-virgin olive oil
- 2 teaspoons lemon juice
- ¼ teaspoon pepper, divided
- ⅛ teaspoon table salt
- 1 cup ½-inch cantaloupe pieces

- ¼ English cucumber, halved lengthwise and sliced thin crosswise (1 cup)
- 2 ounces feta cheese, crumbled (½ cup)
- 2 tablespoons chopped fresh mint

- 2 (6-ounce) boneless, skinless chicken breasts, trimmed
- 4 thin slices prosciutto (2 ounces)
- 2 ounces (2 cups) baby arugula

1 Whisk oil, lemon juice, ⅛ teaspoon pepper, and salt together in large bowl. Add cantaloupe, cucumber, feta, and mint and toss to combine; set aside.

2 Pound chicken between 2 sheets of plastic wrap to uniform thickness. Pat dry with paper towels and sprinkle with remaining ⅛ teaspoon pepper. For each breast, shingle 2 slices of prosciutto on counter, overlapping edges slightly. Lay chicken in center, then wrap prosciutto around chicken.

3 Arrange breasts seam side down in air-fryer basket, spaced evenly apart, alternating ends. Place basket into air fryer and set temperature to 400 degrees. Cook until edges of prosciutto begin to brown and chicken registers 160 degrees, 12 to 18 minutes, flipping chicken halfway through cooking.

4 Add arugula to cantaloupe mixture and toss to combine. Season with salt and pepper to taste. Serve chicken with salad.

Per Serving Cal 470 | Total Fat 24g | Sat Fat 3.5g | Chol 175mg | Sodium 960mg
Total Carb 10g | Dietary Fiber 2g | Total Sugars 8g | Added Sugars 0g | Protein 52g

BROWN SUGAR–BALSAMIC-GLAZED BONE-IN CHICKEN BREAST

Serves 1 to 4 | Total Time: 30 minutes

Why This Recipe Works When cooking for one, roasting a chicken breast in the oven can seem like too much effort. But what if you used your countertop air fryer, which doesn't need preheating? Bone-in chicken air-fries quickly and takes very little prep. We rubbed the breast with a little oil and sprinkled on salt and pepper. Starting the chicken skin side down helped the fat render. We roasted the chicken at 350 degrees, instead of 400, which we often use to quickly air-fry proteins. The lower temperature helped minimize moisture loss. For added flavor, we glazed one side of the breast with a mixture of brown sugar, balsamic vinegar, and garlic. If you plan to discard the chicken skin before serving, reserve the glaze and brush it on the chicken after removing the skin. This recipe is written to serve 1 but can be easily scaled to serve up to 4 people (see page 10).

1 (10- to 12-ounce) bone-in split chicken breast, trimmed

1 teaspoon extra-virgin olive oil

⅛ teaspoon table salt

⅛ teaspoon pepper

2 tablespoons packed brown sugar

2 teaspoons balsamic vinegar

1 small garlic clove, minced to paste

1 Pat chicken dry with paper towels, rub with oil, and sprinkle with salt and pepper. Arrange breast skin side down in air-fryer basket. (Space additional breasts evenly apart, alternating ends.) Place basket into air fryer, set temperature to 350 degrees, and cook for 10 minutes.

2 Microwave sugar, vinegar, and garlic in small bowl until mixture is fluid, about 30 seconds, stirring halfway through microwaving. Flip and rotate breast, then brush with glaze. Return basket to air fryer and cook until chicken is well browned and registers 160 degrees, 15 to 20 minutes. Discard skin, if desired. Let chicken rest for 5 minutes before serving.

PEACH-JALAPEÑO-GLAZED BONE-IN CHICKEN BREAST
Substitute 1 tablespoon peach preserves for sugar, 1 teaspoon lime juice for vinegar, and 2 teaspoons minced jalapeño for garlic.

HONEY-MISO-GLAZED BONE-IN CHICKEN BREAST
Substitute 1 tablespoon honey for sugar, 1 teaspoon unseasoned rice vinegar for balsamic, and 2 teaspoons white or red miso for garlic.

Per Serving (with skin / without skin) Cal 490 / 380 | Total Fat 18 / 9g | Sat Fat 4.5 / 2g | Chol 140 / 115mg
Sodium 400mg | Total Carb 30g | Dietary Fiber 0g | Total Sugars 28g | Added Sugars 27g | Protein 41g

SPICY PEANUT CHICKEN WITH CHARRED GREEN BEANS AND TOMATOES

Serves 2 | Total Time: 1 hour

Why This Recipe Works To give weeknight chicken and vegetables some pizzazz, we developed a peanut-hoisin sauce that was a glaze for the chicken, dressing for the green bean and cherry tomato salad, and sauce for passing at the table. We tossed the green beans with a little oil and air-fried them until they were tender and developed great char. Then we tossed them with tomatoes, scallions, and some peanut sauce. We brushed one side of the chicken with peanut sauce before air frying and glazed the other halfway through cooking, so the meat was well browned and flavorful. For an accurate measurement of boiling water, bring a kettle of water to a boil and then measure out the desired amount. If you plan to discard the chicken skin, do not set aside sauce for brushing in step 1. This recipe can be easily doubled (see page 10).

- ¼ cup boiling water
- 2 tablespoons creamy peanut butter
- 2 tablespoons hoisin sauce
- 1 tablespoon tomato paste
- 1 tablespoon Asian chili-garlic sauce

- 1 pound green beans, trimmed
- 2 teaspoons sesame oil, divided
- 2 (10- to 12-ounce) bone-in split chicken breasts, trimmed
- ¼ teaspoon table salt
- 6 ounces cherry tomatoes, halved

- 3 scallions, sliced thin
- 1 tablespoon chopped dry-roasted unsalted peanuts
- ¼ cup shredded fresh basil
- Lime wedges

1 Whisk boiling water, peanut butter, hoisin, tomato paste, and chili-garlic sauce in bowl until combined; set aside 2 tablespoons sauce for brushing on chicken.

2 Toss green beans with 1 teaspoon oil in large bowl. Arrange in even layer in air-fryer basket. Place basket into air fryer and set temperature to 400 degrees. Cook until green beans are tender and spotty brown, 14 to 19 minutes, tossing halfway through cooking. Return green beans to now-empty bowl; set aside.

3 Pat chicken dry with paper towels, rub with remaining 1 teaspoon oil, and sprinkle with salt. Arrange chicken skin side down in now-empty basket, spaced evenly apart, alternating ends. Place basket into air fryer, set temperature to 350 degrees, and cook for 10 minutes. Flip and rotate chicken, then brush with reserved sauce. Return basket to air fryer and cook until chicken is well browned and registers 160 degrees, 15 to 20 minutes. Transfer chicken to plate and discard skin, if desired. Tent with aluminum foil and let rest while finishing green beans.

4 Add half of remaining sauce, tomatoes, scallions, peanuts, and basil to bowl with green beans and toss to combine. Season with salt and pepper to taste. Serve chicken with salad and lime wedges, passing remaining sauce separately.

Per Serving (with skin / without skin) Cal 620 / 520 | Total Fat 29 / 21g | Sat Fat 6 / 4g | Chol 140 / 115mg Sodium 970 / 950mg | Total Carb 33g | Dietary Fiber 9g | Total Sugars 18g | Added Sugars 0g | Protein 60 / 52g

CHIPOTLE-HONEY FRIED CHICKEN WITH BRUSSELS SPROUT AND CITRUS SALAD

Serves 2 | Total Time: 1 hour

Why This Recipe Works Our air-fryer version of fried chicken is golden and crunchy on the outside and moist and juicy on the inside, just as fried chicken should be. All it needs is a light spray of vegetable oil to cook. The secret was finding a coating that would get crunchy without needing to be deep-fried. In a side-by-side taste test, crushed cornflakes won out over both bread crumbs and Melba toast. To add a punch of smoky spicy flavor, we incorporated chipotle chile in adobo in two ways: in the buttermilk mixture and in an aromatic, warm honey glaze to drizzle on the chicken before serving. For a fresh, healthy accompaniment, we made a salad of shaved brussels sprouts with tangy citrus and a mustard-cider vinaigrette. To crush the cornflakes, place them inside a zipper-lock bag and use a rolling pin or the bottom of a large skillet to break them into fine crumbs.

- 1 orange
- 1 tablespoon extra-virgin olive oil
- 1 tablespoon cider vinegar
- 1 tablespoon whole-grain mustard
- 1 tablespoon honey, divided
- ¼ teaspoon table salt, divided
- ¼ teaspoon pepper, divided
- 8 ounces brussels sprouts, trimmed, halved, and sliced very thin
- Canola oil spray
- ⅓ cup buttermilk
- 2 tablespoons minced canned chipotle chile in adobo sauce, divided
- 1 tablespoon all-purpose flour
- 2 cups (2 ounces) cornflakes, finely crushed
- 1¼ pounds bone-in chicken pieces (split breasts cut in half, drumsticks, and/or thighs), skin removed, trimmed

1 Cut away peel and pith from orange. Quarter orange, then slice crosswise ½ inch thick. Whisk oil, vinegar, mustard, 1 teaspoon honey, ⅛ teaspoon salt, and ⅛ teaspoon pepper together in large bowl. Add brussels sprouts and orange pieces and toss gently to combine; set aside for serving.

2 Lightly spray bottom of air-fryer basket with canola oil spray. Whisk buttermilk, 1 tablespoon chipotle, flour, remaining ⅛ teaspoon salt, and remaining ⅛ teaspoon pepper in medium bowl until smooth. Spread cornflakes in shallow dish.

3 Pat chicken dry with paper towels. Working with 1 piece of chicken at a time, dredge in buttermilk mixture, letting excess drip off, then coat with cornflakes, pressing gently to adhere. Lightly spray chicken pieces with oil spray and arrange in prepared basket, spaced evenly apart. Place basket into air fryer and set temperature to 400 degrees. Cook until chicken is crisp and registers 160 degrees, 15 to 25 minutes, flipping and rotating pieces halfway through cooking.

4 Meanwhile, microwave remaining 1 tablespoon chipotle and remaining 2 teaspoons honey in small bowl until mixture is fluid, about 20 seconds, stirring halfway through microwaving. Drizzle chicken with chipotle mixture and serve with salad.

Per Serving Cal 510 | Total Fat 13g | Sat Fat 2.5g | Chol 115mg | Sodium 780mg
Total Carb 48g | Dietary Fiber 6g | Total Sugars 20g | Added Sugars 8g | Protein 49g

ROASTED CHICKEN THIGHS WITH POTATOES AND MESCLUN SALAD

Serves 2 | Total Time: 1 hour

Why This Recipe Works What's more satisfying than juicy, crispy-skinned chicken and perfectly cooked potatoes? For our updated healthier version of the bistro classic, we air-fried the chicken and russets together and offset their richness with a bright salad. Bone-in chicken thighs hold their shape after roasting, and the dark meat becomes superflavorful. We used a skewer to poke holes in the chicken skin to allow the fat to render during cooking, then roasted the chicken on top of the potatoes, which we tossed with fragrant ground coriander, olive oil, salt, and pepper. Chicken juices added more flavor as they dripped onto the potatoes. When the chicken was well browned, we rested it while crisping the potatoes. Mesclun, radishes, and scallions in a tangy tarragon-mustard dressing brought freshness to the plate. The dressing also served as a sauce for the chicken. If you plan to discard the chicken skin, skip poking with skewer. This recipe can be easily doubled (see page 10).

12 ounces russet potatoes, unpeeled, cut into 1-inch wedges

1 teaspoon plus 2 tablespoons extra-virgin olive oil, divided

½ teaspoon ground coriander

½ teaspoon table salt, divided

½ teaspoon pepper, divided

2 (5- to 7-ounce) bone-in chicken thighs, trimmed

1 tablespoon lemon juice

1 teaspoon minced fresh thyme

1 teaspoon Dijon mustard

¼ cup minced fresh tarragon, basil, dill, and/or parsley, divided

5 ounces (5 cups) mesclun

2 radishes, trimmed and sliced thin

2 scallions, sliced thin

1 Toss potatoes with 1 teaspoon oil, coriander, ¼ teaspoon salt, and ¼ teaspoon pepper in large bowl. Arrange potatoes in even layer in air-fryer basket; do not clean bowl.

2 Using metal skewer, poke skin side of chicken 10 to 15 times. Pat chicken dry with paper towels and sprinkle with remaining ¼ teaspoon salt and ¼ teaspoon pepper. Arrange chicken skin side up on top of potatoes, spaced evenly apart. Place basket into air fryer; set temperature to 350 degrees; and cook until potatoes are tender and chicken is well browned and crisp and registers 195 degrees, 30 to 40 minutes, tossing potatoes and rotating chicken halfway through cooking (do not flip chicken).

3 Transfer chicken to clean plate and discard skin, if desired. Tent with aluminum foil and let rest while finishing potatoes and salad. Return basket to air fryer and increase temperature to 400 degrees. Cook potatoes until golden brown and crisp, 6 to 10 minutes.

4 Whisk remaining 2 tablespoons oil, lemon juice, thyme, and mustard together in large bowl; stir in tarragon. Spoon 2 tablespoons dressing over chicken. Add mesclun, radishes, and scallions to bowl with remaining dressing and toss to coat. Season with salt and pepper to taste. Serve chicken with potatoes and salad.

Per Serving (with skin / without skin) Cal 510 / 440 | Total Fat 29 / 22g | Sat Fat 6 / 4g | Chol 110 / 90mg
Sodium 740 / 730mg | Total Carb 34g | Dietary Fiber 3g | Total Sugars 2g | Added Sugars 0g | Protein 23 / 21g

CHICKEN THIGHS WITH ROASTED MUSHROOMS AND TOMATOES

Serves 2 | Total Time: 45 minutes

Why This Recipe Works These chicken thighs roasted on a pile of vegetables are so easy and flavorful they'll become a regular on your weeknight calendar. We roasted skin-on chicken thighs (the skin poked with a skewer) directly on top of mushrooms, tomatoes, and garlic cloves. The chicken juices flavored the vegetables while the rendered fat fell through the basket, leaving the dish grease-free. There's one chicken thigh per person, but the portobellos added heft. Rosemary's floral flavor contributed aromatic notes, paying homage to classic cacciatore. The short roasting process transformed even off-season tomatoes into concentrated goodness and the garlic cloves to melt-in-your-mouth perfection. A splash of sherry vinegar and fresh basil finished the dish with brightness. If you plan to discard the chicken skin, skip poking with a skewer. This recipe can be easily doubled (see page 10).

- 12 ounces portobello mushroom caps, gills removed, cut into 2-inch pieces
- 4 plum tomatoes, cored and halved lengthwise
- 6 garlic cloves, lightly crushed and peeled
- 2 tablespoons extra-virgin olive oil
- 1½ teaspoons minced fresh rosemary
- ½ teaspoon table salt, divided
- ½ teaspoon pepper, divided
- ⅛ teaspoon red pepper flakes
- 2 (5- to 7-ounce) bone-in, skin-on chicken thighs, trimmed
- 1 tablespoon sherry vinegar
- 2 tablespoons chopped fresh basil

1 Toss mushrooms and tomatoes with garlic, oil, rosemary, ¼ teaspoon salt, ¼ teaspoon pepper, and pepper flakes. Transfer to air-fryer basket and spread into even layer.

2 Using metal skewer, poke skin side of chicken 10 to 15 times. Pat chicken dry with paper towels and sprinkle with remaining ¼ teaspoon salt and remaining ¼ teaspoon pepper. Arrange chicken skin side up on top of vegetables, spaced evenly apart. Place basket into air fryer and set temperature to 400 degrees. Cook until vegetables are browned and chicken is well browned and crisp and registers 195 degrees, 25 to 35 minutes, stirring vegetables and rotating chicken halfway through cooking (do not flip chicken).

3 Transfer chicken to plate and discard skin, if desired. Tent with aluminum foil and let rest for 5 minutes. Transfer vegetables to serving platter and season with salt and pepper to taste. Drizzle with vinegar and sprinkle with basil. Serve chicken with vegetables.

Per Serving (with skin / without skin) Cal 390 / 320 | Total Fat 27 / 20g | Sat Fat 5 / 3.5g | Chol 110 / 90mg
Sodium 690 / 680mg | Total Carb 15g | Dietary Fiber 4g | Total Sugars 7g | Added Sugars 0g | Protein 24 / 22g

CORIANDER CHICKEN THIGHS WITH ROASTED CAULIFLOWER AND SHALLOTS

Serves 2 | Total Time: 1 hour

Why This Recipe Works The fragrance of lemony-coconutty coriander seed is so potent, we wanted to use it in several ways for this dish, which contains more vegetables—cauliflower, shallots, and tomatoes—than chicken. We seasoned the vegetables and the protein with ground coriander, creating a flavorful spice crust, and also added the spice to the citrusy dressing. Toasting and grinding coriander seeds right before using ensured the freshest flavor. Cutting the cauliflower into 2-inch florets meant the cauliflower cooked in the same amount of time as the chicken. Poking holes in the chicken thighs with a skewer helped render the fat as they cook; cooking them skin side up made the skin golden and crisp. Toast coriander seeds in a dry skillet over medium heat until fragrant (about 2 minutes), and then remove the skillet from the heat so that the coriander won't scorch. If you plan to discard the chicken skin, skip poking with skewer. Instead, loosen skin covering thighs and rub coriander mixture under skin. This recipe can be easily doubled (see page 10).

- 2 teaspoons coriander seeds, toasted
- ½ teaspoon paprika
- ½ teaspoon table salt
- ½ teaspoon pepper
- 1 pound cauliflower florets, cut into 2-inch pieces
- 2 shallots, peeled and quartered
- 2 tablespoons extra-virgin olive oil, divided
- 1½ tablespoons lime juice
- 1 small garlic clove, finely grated
- 2 (5- to 7-ounce) bone-in, skin-on chicken thighs, trimmed
- 8 ounces cherry tomatoes, halved
- ⅓ cup chopped fresh cilantro

1 Crush coriander in mortar and pestle or spice grinder until coarsely ground; transfer to small bowl. Stir in paprika, salt, and pepper.

2 Toss cauliflower and shallots with 1 tablespoon oil and 1 teaspoon coriander mixture in large bowl. Transfer to air-fryer basket and spread into even layer. Combine lime juice, garlic, 1 teaspoon coriander mixture, and remaining 1 tablespoon oil in now-empty bowl; set aside.

3 Using metal skewer, poke skin side of chicken 10 to 15 times. Pat chicken dry with paper towels and rub evenly with remaining coriander mixture. Arrange chicken skin side up on top of vegetables, spaced evenly apart. Place basket into air fryer and set temperature to 400 degrees. Cook until vegetables are tender and chicken is well browned and crisp and registers 195 degrees, 25 to 35 minutes, stirring vegetables and rotating chicken halfway through cooking (do not flip chicken).

4 Transfer chicken to plate and let rest for 5 minutes.
Transfer vegetables to bowl with lime juice–garlic mixture.
Add tomatoes and cilantro and toss to coat. Season with salt
and pepper to taste. Serve chicken with vegetables.

Per Serving (with skin / without skin) Cal 410 / 340 | Total Fat 27 / 21g | Sat Fat 6 / 4g | Chol 110 / 90mg
Sodium 740 / 730mg | Total Carb 19g | Dietary Fiber 7g | Total Sugars 8g | Added Sugars 0g | Protein 25 / 23g

SPICED CHICKEN KEBABS WITH VEGETABLE AND BULGUR SALAD

Serves 2 | Total Time: 1 hour

Why This Recipe Works For this recipe, we used skewers to raise the vegetables and chicken in the air fryer, allowing heat to circulate around them to generate better browning and charring for both. Partway through cooking, we stacked the chicken kebabs on the vegetable kebabs, placed crosswise for maximum air circulation, bringing the chicken closer to the heat source. A garlicky yogurt mixture spiced with baharat, an East Mediterranean spice blend, acted as a marinade for the chicken and sauce for the finished dish. Using bigger pieces of chicken and packing them tightly onto skewers kept the meat juicy. Skewering the vegetables separately allowed us to tailor cooking times so that the chicken and vegetables were ready at the same time. The vegetables retained their great charred flavor even after being chopped further for the bulgur salad. Look for medium-grind bulgur (labeled "#2"), which is roughly the size of mustard seeds. Avoid coarsely ground bulgur; it will not cook through in time. If you can't find baharat, you can substitute ½ teaspoon paprika, ¼ teaspoon pepper, ⅛ teaspoon ground cumin, and pinch ground cloves. Serve with warmed pitas or naans, if desired. This recipe can be easily doubled (see page 10).

½ cup medium-grind bulgur, rinsed

⅓ cup boiling water

1 teaspoon baharat, divided

½ teaspoon table salt, divided

⅔ cup plain Greek yogurt

2 teaspoons grated lemon zest plus ¼ cup lemon juice, divided (2 lemons)

2 tablespoons extra-virgin olive oil, divided

1 small garlic clove, minced to paste

12 ounces boneless, skinless chicken breasts, trimmed and cut into 1½-inch pieces

½ cup coarsely chopped fresh mint, divided

½ cup coarsely chopped fresh parsley, divided

1 small red bell pepper, stemmed, seeded, and cut into 1½-inch pieces

1 small red onion, halved and cut through root end into 6 equal wedges

Olive oil spray

5 (6-inch) wooden skewers

2 tablespoons toasted chopped pistachios, almonds, or walnuts

1 Combine bulgur, boiling water, ¾ teaspoon baharat, and ¼ teaspoon salt in large bowl. Cover tightly with plastic wrap and let sit while preparing kebabs.

2 Combine yogurt, lemon zest, 2 tablespoons lemon juice, 1 tablespoon oil, garlic, remaining ¼ teaspoon baharat, and remaining ¼ teaspoon salt in bowl. Transfer ¼ cup yogurt mixture to medium bowl, add chicken, and toss to coat; let marinate for at least 15 minutes or up to 1 hour. Stir ¼ cup mint and ¼ cup parsley into remaining yogurt mixture and season with salt and pepper to taste; set aside for serving.

3 Thread bell pepper and onion evenly onto 3 skewers; lightly spray with oil spray. Arrange kebabs in air-fryer basket, parallel to each other and spaced evenly apart. Place basket into air fryer, set temperature to 375 degrees, and cook for 5 minutes.

4 Meanwhile, thread chicken evenly onto remaining 2 skewers. Arrange chicken kebabs on top of vegetable kebabs, perpendicular to bottom layer. Return basket to air fryer and cook until chicken is lightly browned and registers 160 degrees, 15 to 20 minutes, flipping and rotating chicken kebabs halfway through cooking. Transfer chicken kebabs to plate, tent with aluminum foil, and let rest while finishing salad.

5 Transfer vegetable kebabs to cutting board. When cool enough to handle, slide vegetables off skewers and chop coarse. Add vegetables, pistachios, remaining 2 tablespoons lemon juice, remaining 1 tablespoon oil, remaining ¼ cup mint, and remaining ¼ cup parsley to bulgur and toss to combine. Season with salt and pepper to taste. Serve chicken kebabs and salad with yogurt sauce.

Per Serving Cal 590 | Total Fat 24g | Sat Fat 4.5g | Chol 130mg | Sodium 700mg
Total Carb 42g | Dietary Fiber 8g | Total Sugars 8g | Added Sugars 0g | Protein 52g

CHICKEN AND CHICKPEA SALAD WITH CARROTS, CUCUMBERS, AND FETA

Serves 2 | Total Time: 30 minutes

Why This Recipe Works This quick and easy protein-packed salad combines tender chicken, crunchy chickpeas, and vegetables. We tossed the chicken and chickpeas in a smoked paprika mixture (which we also used in our dressing) before air-frying them together. This took the chickpeas from soft and creamy to slightly crispy and firm, and cooked the chicken to a golden brown. Shredded carrots provided a sweet orange foil to the meat and legumes, and Persian (aka "mini") cucumbers added green color and coolness. We loved the "use up what you have on hand" approach of this recipe toward nuts and herbs. Use mint, cilantro, or parsley, or any combination of these. We added toasted almonds but you could use other nuts. Finally, feta added creamy tartness. Use the large holes on a box grater to shred the carrots. Use half an English cucumber if you can't find Persian ones. For more information on toasting nuts in the air fryer, see page 12. This recipe can be easily doubled (see page 10).

- 2 tablespoons extra-virgin olive oil
- 2 garlic cloves, minced
- 1 teaspoon smoked paprika
- ⅛ teaspoon table salt
- 12 ounces boneless, skinless chicken breasts, trimmed and cut into 1-inch pieces

- 1 (15-ounce) can chickpeas, rinsed
- 2 tablespoons lemon juice
- 2 carrots, peeled and shredded
- 2 Persian cucumbers, sliced thin

- ½ cup chopped fresh mint, cilantro, and/or parsley
- 1 ounce feta cheese, cut into ½-inch pieces (¼ cup)
- 2 tablespoons chopped toasted almonds

1 Microwave oil, garlic, paprika, and salt in large bowl until fragrant, about 1 minute, stirring halfway through microwaving.

2 Toss chicken and chickpeas with 2 teaspoons oil mixture. Transfer to air-fryer basket and spread into even layer. Place basket into air fryer and set temperature to 400 degrees. Cook until chicken registers 160 degrees, 10 to 15 minutes, stirring halfway through cooking.

3 Whisk lemon juice into remaining oil mixture. Add chicken and chickpeas, carrots, cucumbers, mint, feta, and almonds and toss gently to combine. Season with salt and pepper to taste. Serve.

Per Serving Cal 600 | Total Fat 29g | Sat Fat 6g | Chol 135mg | Sodium 810mg
Total Carb 34g | Dietary Fiber 11g | Total Sugars 6g | Added Sugars 0g | Protein 51g

HOISIN-GINGER CHICKEN SALAD WITH NAPA CABBAGE, SHIITAKES, AND BELL PEPPER

Serves 2 | Total Time: 45 minutes

Why This Recipe Works The air fryer's intense circulating heat creates the perfect condition for sealing in the juices and flavors of chicken thighs (and other meats). These same conditions help generate even, deeply burnished glazes. The trick is to use a glaze that isn't too thick (which can become gloppy) or too thin (which can slide off), and to add it at the right time so that it doesn't burn before the meat reaches the proper temperature—that time is when the meat is parcooked. We thinned store-bought hoisin sauce with fragrant ginger and a splash of vinegar, which also added welcome brightness and acidity to the sweet and savory hoisin. We first cooked the chicken on a layer of shiitake mushrooms, which steamed while absorbing flavorful chicken juices. Then we brushed on some glaze and continued to cook the chicken. By the time the chicken reached the correct temperature, the glaze had reduced and adhered to the thighs. We glazed the second side, and after a few more minutes in the air fryer, our chicken and shiitakes were ready to be sliced into a hearty topping for a colorful salad with napa cabbage, bell pepper, scallions, cilantro, and peanuts. You can substitute sliced romaine lettuce for the napa cabbage. This recipe can be easily doubled (see page 10).

4 teaspoons toasted sesame oil, divided

2 tablespoons unseasoned rice vinegar, divided

1 tablespoon grated fresh ginger, divided

2 teaspoons soy sauce

4 cups thinly sliced napa cabbage

1 small red bell pepper, stemmed, seeded, and cut into ¼-inch-wide strips

2 scallions, sliced thin on bias

4 ounces shiitake mushrooms, stemmed

12 ounces boneless, skinless chicken thighs, trimmed

3 tablespoons hoisin sauce

¼ cup fresh cilantro leaves

¼ cup unsalted dry-roasted peanuts

1 Whisk 1 tablespoon oil, 1 tablespoon vinegar, 1 teaspoon ginger, and soy sauce together in large bowl. Add cabbage, bell pepper, and scallions and toss to combine; set aside.

2 Toss mushrooms with remaining 1 teaspoon oil and arrange gill side up in even layer in air-fryer basket. Pat chicken dry with paper towels and arrange in even layer on top of mushrooms. Place basket into air fryer, set temperature to 400 degrees, and cook for 5 minutes.

3 Whisk hoisin, remaining 1 tablespoon vinegar, and remaining 2 teaspoons ginger together in small bowl. Brush tops of chicken thighs with half of hoisin mixture. Return basket to air fryer and cook until chicken is well browned and registers 175 degrees, 10 to 15 minutes. Flip chicken; brush with remaining hoisin mixture; and cook until glaze is bubbly, about 2 minutes.

4 Transfer chicken and mushrooms to cutting board, let cool slightly, then slice thin. Toss cabbage mixture to recombine and season with salt and pepper to taste. Divide salad among individual serving bowls and top with chicken, mushrooms, cilantro, and peanuts. Serve.

Per Serving Cal 540 | Total Fat 29g | Sat Fat 5g | Chol 160mg | Sodium 890mg
Total Carb 26g | Dietary Fiber 6g | Total Sugars 13g | Added Sugars 0g | Protein 43g

CHICKEN-TOMATILLO TACOS WITH ROASTED PINEAPPLE SALSA

Serves 2 | Total Time: 1 hour

Why This Recipe Works The chicken filling for tacos is often simmered. But if overcooked, the meat dries out, so to ensure that our chicken stayed juicy and flavorful, we used chicken thighs instead of breasts. We were also excited to use the air fryer for the other elements of the dish: roasting tomatillos and the ingredients for a deeply flavorful fruit salsa. We kept the seasoning on the chicken and tomatillos simple because this salsa has it all: poblanos for heat, red onion for zip, and pineapple for sweetness. We found that the air fryer heightened the pineapple's yellow color and enhanced its sweetness. Roasting the chicken on a bed of tomatillos allowed the chicken juices to saturate the tomatillos while their skins charred and started to break down. The tartness of the tomatillos complemented the sweet pineapple salsa, and a garnish of thinly sliced radishes and queso fresco brought crunch and richness to the tacos. If fresh tomatillos are unavailable, substitute one (11-ounce) can of tomatillos, drained, rinsed, and patted dry. You can lightly char the tortillas one at a time over a gas burner or stack tortillas, wrap tightly in aluminum foil, and warm in the air fryer set to 350 degrees for 5 minutes, flipping halfway through cooking. This recipe can be easily doubled (see page 10).

- 2 poblano chiles, stemmed, quartered, and seeded
- 2 jalapeño chiles, stemmed, halved, and seeded (optional)
- 1 small red onion, quartered
- 1 cup 1-inch fresh or thawed frozen pineapple pieces
- 1 tablespoon extra-virgin olive oil, divided
- ¼ teaspoon table salt, divided
- ¼ teaspoon pepper, divided
- ½ cup coarsely chopped fresh cilantro
- 1 tablespoon lime juice, plus lime wedges for serving
- 12 ounces tomatillos, husks and stems removed, rinsed well, patted dry, and halved
- 12 ounces boneless, skinless chicken thighs, trimmed
- 6 (6-inch) corn tortillas, warmed
- 1 ounce queso fresco, crumbled (¼ cup)
- 2 radishes, trimmed and sliced thin

1 Toss poblanos; jalapeños, if using; onion; and pineapple with 2 teaspoons oil, ⅛ teaspoon salt, and ⅛ teaspoon pepper in bowl. Transfer to air-fryer basket and spread into even layer; do not clean bowl.

2 Place basket into air fryer and set temperature to 400 degrees. Cook until chile-pineapple mixture is tender and spotty brown, 15 to 20 minutes, stirring halfway through cooking. Transfer mixture to cutting board, let cool slightly, then chop coarse. Combine chile-pineapple

mixture, cilantro, and lime juice in bowl and season with salt and pepper to taste; set aside for serving.

3 Toss tomatillos with remaining 1 teaspoon oil and arrange in even layer in now-empty basket. Pat chicken dry with paper towels and sprinkle with remaining ⅛ teaspoon salt, and remaining ⅛ teaspoon pepper. Arrange chicken on top of tomatillos, spaced evenly apart. Return

basket to air fryer and cook until tomatillos are blistered and chicken registers 175 degrees, 15 to 20 minutes, flipping and rotating chicken halfway through cooking.

4 Transfer chicken to cutting board, let cool slightly, then shred into bite-size pieces using 2 forks. Serve chicken and tomatillos with warmed tortillas, passing salsa, queso fresco, radishes, and extra lime wedges separately.

Per Serving Cal 640 | Total Fat 22g | Sat Fat 5g | Chol 170mg | Sodium 720mg
Total Carb 69g | Dietary Fiber 5g | Total Sugars 23g | Added Sugars 0g | Protein 44g

ROASTED CHICKEN SAUSAGES WITH BUTTERNUT SQUASH AND RADICCHIO

Serves 2 | Total Time: 45 minutes

Why This Recipe Works For a quick, easy dinner, sausages can't be beat. Pairing them with hearty, sweet butternut squash gave us a satisfying meal. The squash got a 10-minute head start in the air fryer so that it was fully tender by the time the sausages were cooked through. A swipe of honey helped speed up the browning of the sausage, which stayed juicy on the inside. Bitter radicchio added bulk and balanced out the sweet roasted squash, a cider vinegar–honey dressing tied everything together, and toasted walnuts added crunch. Chicken sausage is available in a variety of flavors; feel free to use any flavor that you think will work well in this dish. Turkey sausage can be substituted for the chicken sausage. For more information on toasting nuts in the air fryer, see page 12. This recipe can be easily doubled (see page 10).

1½ pounds butternut squash, peeled, seeded, and cut into 1-inch pieces (4 cups)

4 teaspoons extra-virgin olive oil, divided, plus extra for drizzling

½ teaspoon minced fresh thyme or ⅛ teaspoon dried

⅛ teaspoon table salt

Pinch cayenne pepper (optional)

6 ounces raw chicken sausage (2 sausages)

2 teaspoons honey, warmed, divided

2 teaspoons cider vinegar

1 teaspoon Dijon mustard

¼ teaspoon pepper

½ small head radicchio (3 ounces), cored and sliced ½ inch thick

2 tablespoons chopped toasted walnuts

2 tablespoons chopped fresh basil or parsley

1 Toss squash with 2 teaspoons oil; thyme; salt; and cayenne, if using. Transfer to air-fryer basket and spread into even layer. Place basket into air fryer; set temperature to 400 degrees; and cook until beginning to brown, 10 to 15 minutes, stirring halfway through cooking.

2 Brush sausages with 1 teaspoon honey. Stir squash, then arrange sausages on top, spaced evenly apart. Return basket to air fryer and cook until squash is tender and sausages are lightly browned and register 165 degrees, 8 to 13 minutes, flipping and rotating sausages halfway through cooking.

3 Transfer sausages to plate and let rest while finishing squash. Whisk vinegar, mustard, pepper, remaining 2 teaspoons oil, and remaining 1 teaspoon honey together in large bowl. Add squash, radicchio, walnuts, and basil and toss to coat. Season with salt and pepper to taste. Serve sausages with vegetables.

Per Serving Cal 510 | Total Fat 29g | Sat Fat 5g | Chol 135mg | Sodium 770mg
Total Carb 50g | Dietary Fiber 8g | Total Sugars 13g | Added Sugars 5g | Protein 18g

WHOLE ROAST CHICKEN WITH LEMON, DILL, AND GARLIC

Serves 4 | Total Time: 1½ hours

Why This Recipe Works Cooking space is compact even in larger air fryers (one of the reasons foods cook so evenly) but with a few adjustments, we were able to roast a whole chicken successfully. The convection heat helped seal the exterior and lock in flavors and juices while creating a golden layer of crackly-crisp skin. To ensure that our bird fit in the air fryer with room for good air circulation, we did two things: First, we forewent the usual step of tying the legs, as this tends to increase the chicken's height. Leaving them untied allowed for greater air circulation and faster cooking around the legs and thighs, which needed to cook to a higher temperature than the breast meat. Next, we pressed down gently on the breast so that it would sit flatter in the air fryer. We started the chicken breast side down, which gave the legs a jump start. Halfway through cooking, we flipped the chicken breast side up, so the breast meat and skin could finish to perfection. Finally, we created several aromatic blends to rub underneath the skin (we found that aromatics rubbed on the outside quickly burned). We had the best success with chickens weighing between 3½ and 4 pounds; larger chickens will require increased cooking time and may not fit in your air fryer. For a simpler roast, skip the aromatics and simply season the outside of the chicken with salt and pepper. You will need an air fryer with at least a 6-quart capacity for this recipe. If using an air-fryer lid for a multicooker, do not use basket insert; place chicken directly into pot.

- 1 tablespoon extra-virgin olive oil
- 2 teaspoons grated lemon zest
- 2 teaspoons dried dill weed
- ½ teaspoon garlic powder
- ½ teaspoon table salt
- ¼ teaspoon pepper
- 1 (3½- to 4-pound) whole chicken, giblets discarded

1 Combine oil, lemon zest, dill, garlic, salt, and pepper in small bowl. Pat chicken dry with paper towels. Use your fingers to gently loosen skin covering breast and thighs. Carefully spoon spice mixture under skin, directly on meat on each side of breast and on thighs. Distribute spices over meat gently with fingertips. Arrange chicken breast side up in center of cutting board and, using heels of palms, firmly press on breast to flatten slightly.

2 Arrange chicken breast side down in air-fryer basket. Place basket into air fryer and set temperature to 400 degrees. Cook until chicken is light golden brown and skin is lightly crisped, about 30 minutes.

3 Using tongs, flip chicken breast side up. Return basket to air fryer and continue to cook chicken until breasts register 160 degrees and thighs register 175 degrees, 15 to 30 minutes.

4 Transfer chicken to carving board and let rest for 15 minutes. Carve chicken, discarding skin, if desired. Serve.

WHOLE ROAST CHICKEN WITH ORANGE, ALEPPO, AND CINNAMON

Substitute orange zest for lemon zest, ground dried Aleppo pepper for dill, and cinnamon for garlic.

WHOLE ROAST CHICKEN WITH GINGER, CUMIN, AND CARDAMOM

Substitute grated fresh ginger for lemon zest, ground cumin for dill, and ground cardamom for garlic.

Per Serving (with skin / without skin) Cal 490 / 280 | Total Fat 29 / 13g | Sat Fat 8 / 3g | Chol 165 / 115mg
Sodium 450 / 400mg | Total Carb 1g | Dietary Fiber 0g | Total Sugars 0g | Added Sugars 0g | Protein 52 / 37g

BEEF AND PORK

72 Roasted Steak Tips with Tomatoes and Gorgonzola

75 Lemon-Sage Top Sirloin Steak with Roasted Carrots and Shallots

76 Top Sirloin Steak with Roasted Zucchini and Shiitakes

78 Steak Frites

81 Flank Steak with Corn and Black Bean Salad

82 Dill-and-Coriander-Rubbed Roasted Pork Chop
Barbecue-Rubbed Roasted Pork Chop
Herb-Rubbed Roasted Pork Chop

84 Crispy Pork Chops with Roasted Peach, Blackberry, and Arugula Salad

86 Sweet and Spicy Glazed Pork Chops with Sesame Bok Choy

89 Roasted Bone-In Pork Chop with Sweet Potatoes and Maple-Rosemary Sauce

90 Lemon-Thyme Pork Tenderloin with Green Beans and Hazelnuts

92 Marinated Pork Gyros

ROASTED STEAK TIPS WITH TOMATOES AND GORGONZOLA

Serves 2 | Total Time: 30 minutes

Why This Recipe Works When steak calls your name, an air fryer can be the answer. Steak tips roasted in the appliance quickly yield lean, tender meat with rich flavor and fabulous color. Eight to 12 ounces of steak tips, cut into 2-inch pieces, fit easily in the chamber but there is room for up to 1½ pounds. Seasoning the steak with salt and pepper allowed its beefiness to shine. We coated the meat with a little oil to keep it from drying out in the high heat. As the steak rested (to allow its juices to distribute evenly and to relax the meat), we made a salad with tomatoes, tangy dressing, and a sprinkle of Gorgonzola. Sirloin steak tips, also called flap meat, are sold as whole steaks, strips, and cubes. To ensure uniform pieces, we prefer to purchase whole steak tips and cut them ourselves. If only strips are available, look for relatively even, 1-inch-thick pieces, and cut them into 2-inch lengths. For the best results, use peak-of-the-season tomatoes. This recipe can be easily doubled (see page 10).

2 teaspoons red wine vinegar

½ teaspoon Dijon mustard

½ teaspoon table salt, divided

½ teaspoon pepper, divided

1 small shallot, sliced thin

8-12 ounces sirloin steak tips, trimmed and cut into 2-inch pieces

4 teaspoons extra-virgin olive oil, divided

1 tablespoon chopped fresh parsley

1 pound mixed tomatoes, cored

2 tablespoons crumbled Gorgonzola cheese

1 Whisk vinegar, mustard, ¼ teaspoon salt, and ¼ teaspoon pepper together in small bowl; stir in shallot and set aside.

2 Toss steak tips with 1 teaspoon oil, remaining ¼ teaspoon salt, and remaining ¼ teaspoon pepper. Arrange steak tips in air-fryer basket, spaced evenly apart. Place basket into air fryer and set temperature to 400 degrees. Cook until steak tips are lightly browned and register 130 to 135 degrees (for medium), 12 to 18 minutes, flipping and rotating steak tips halfway through cooking.

3 Transfer steak tips to plate, tent with aluminum foil, and let rest for 5 minutes. Meanwhile, whisk parsley and remaining 1 tablespoon oil into vinegar mixture. Halve or quarter small tomatoes, cut medium tomatoes into ½-inch wedges, and slice large tomatoes ¼ inch thick. Arrange tomatoes attractively on serving platter, spoon dressing over top, and sprinkle with Gorgonzola. Serve steak tips with tomato salad.

Per Serving Cal 380 | Total Fat 23g | Sat Fat 7g | Chol 95mg | Sodium 780mg
Total Carb 10g | Dietary Fiber 3g | Total Sugars 6g | Added Sugars 0g | Protein 34g

LEMON-SAGE TOP SIRLOIN STEAK WITH ROASTED CARROTS AND SHALLOTS

Serves 2 | Total Time: 45 minutes

Why This Recipe Works The key to this dinner was to combine some flavorful ingredients (earthy carrots; piquant shallots; and beefy, lean sirloin) with aromatic complements (sage, lemon, and olive oil) and to nail the order of operations, using the air fryer's intense, even heat to bring out the best in the ingredients. First we roasted carrots and halved shallots till they were just softened. Then we transferred them to a bowl and tossed them simply with lemon zest, separately coating the steak in sage and lemon zest. The time it took to cook the steak perfectly was just right for roasting the coating gently without burning it. While the steak rested, we finished air-frying the vegetables so that they would be spotty brown, tender, and warm when it was time to eat. This recipe can be easily doubled using two steaks (see page 10).

- 1 pound carrots, peeled and halved crosswise, thicker pieces halved lengthwise
- 6 shallots, halved through root end
- 1 tablespoon extra-virgin olive oil, divided
- ½ teaspoon table salt, divided
- ¼ teaspoon pepper, divided
- 1 tablespoon grated lemon zest, divided, plus lemon wedges for serving
- 1 tablespoon minced fresh sage
- 1 (8- to 12-ounce) top sirloin steak, 1½ inches thick, trimmed

1 Toss carrots and shallots with 2 teaspoons oil, ¼ teaspoon salt, and ⅛ teaspoon pepper in large bowl. Arrange vegetables in even layer in air-fryer basket. Place basket into air fryer and set temperature to 400 degrees. Cook until vegetables are softened, 8 to 10 minutes. Return vegetables to bowl and toss gently with 1½ teaspoons lemon zest; cover to keep warm.

2 Combine sage, remaining 1 teaspoon oil, remaining ¼ teaspoon salt, remaining ⅛ teaspoon pepper, and remaining 1½ teaspoons lemon zest in bowl. Pat steak dry with paper towels and rub with sage mixture. Place steak in now-empty basket, return basket to air fryer, and set temperature to 400 degrees. Cook until steak is lightly browned and registers 120 to 125 degrees (for medium-rare) or 130 to 135 degrees (for medium), 14 to 20 minutes, flipping and rotating steak halfway through cooking.

3 Transfer steak to cutting board, tent with aluminum foil, and let rest while finishing vegetables. Return vegetables to basket. Place basket into air fryer; set temperature to 400 degrees; and cook until vegetables are tender and spotty brown, 3 to 5 minutes. Slice steak thin and serve with vegetables and lemon wedges.

Per Serving Cal 350 | Total Fat 13g | Sat Fat 3g | Chol 60mg | Sodium 780mg
Total Carb 34g | Dietary Fiber 9g | Total Sugars 16g | Added Sugars 0g | Protein 26g

TOP SIRLOIN STEAK WITH ROASTED ZUCCHINI AND SHIITAKES

Serves 2 | Total Time: 1 hour

Why This Recipe Works For a dinner inspired by Japanese flavors, we paired steak with zucchini and shiitakes flavored with umami-rich miso, garlic, and scallions. We tossed the vegetables with potent toasted sesame oil and gave them a head start in the air fryer to prevent overcrowding the air-fryer basket and steaming the steak. We roasted the zucchini in larger pieces so that it could brown but not overcook or get mushy. Then we removed the zucchini and mushrooms and cooked the steak till it was lightly browned. While the meat rested, we made a miso dressing, sliced the zucchini into smaller pieces, and tossed it with the mushrooms and the dressing. You can serve this dish with brown rice or quinoa. This recipe can be easily doubled (see page 10).

- 12 ounces shiitake mushrooms, stemmed, halved if large
- 2 scallions, white parts cut into 1-inch lengths, green parts sliced thin
- 1 tablespoon toasted sesame oil, divided
- ½ teaspoon table salt, divided
- 2 small zucchini (6 ounces each), halved lengthwise
- 1 (8- to 12-ounce) top sirloin steak, 1½ inches thick, trimmed
- 1 tablespoon canola oil, divided
- 1 tablespoon white miso
- 1 tablespoon warm tap water
- 2 tablespoons mirin
- 1 garlic clove, minced to paste
- ¼ teaspoon white pepper

1 Toss mushrooms and scallion whites with 1 teaspoon sesame oil and ⅛ teaspoon salt in large bowl. Arrange mushroom mixture in even layer in air-fryer basket. Toss zucchini with 1 teaspoon sesame oil and ⅛ teaspoon salt in now-empty bowl. Arrange zucchini cut side up on top of mushroom mixture, spaced evenly apart.

2 Place basket into air fryer and set temperature to 400 degrees. Cook until vegetables are softened and lightly browned, 15 to 20 minutes. Transfer zucchini to cutting board and mushroom mixture to now-empty bowl; cover to keep warm.

3 Pat steak dry with paper towels, rub with 1 teaspoon canola oil, and sprinkle with remaining ¼ teaspoon salt. Place steak in now-empty basket; return basket to air fryer; and cook until steak is lightly browned and registers 120 to 125 degrees (for medium-rare) or 130 to 135 degrees (for medium), 12 to 18 minutes, flipping and rotating steak halfway through cooking. Transfer steak to cutting board with zucchini, tent with aluminum foil, and let rest for 5 minutes.

4 Meanwhile, whisk miso and warm tap water in small bowl until miso is dissolved. Whisk in mirin, garlic, white pepper, remaining 1 teaspoon sesame oil, and remaining 2 teaspoons canola oil. Slice zucchini 1 inch thick. Add zucchini, scallion greens, and 1 tablespoon dressing to bowl with mushroom mixture and toss gently to combine. Season with salt and pepper to taste. Slice steak thin and serve with mushroom-zucchini mixture, passing remaining dressing separately.

Per Serving Cal 480 | Total Fat 23g | Sat Fat 4.5g | Chol 90mg | Sodium 910mg
Total Carb 26g | Dietary Fiber 6g | Total Sugars 11g | Added Sugars 0g | Protein 42g

STEAK FRITES

Serves 2 | Total Time: 1 hour

Why This Recipe Works Sometimes you just want to eat meat and fried potatoes. How do you do that in a healthy way? Use lean meat, don't actually deep-fry the potatoes, and cook in an air fryer. To tweak this French bistro classic, we air-fried the meat and frites together. For the steak, using thicker sirloin meant that we got nice color on the meat while the middle stayed tender and juicy. Making crispy fries with fluffy interiors required a three-step process: a rinse and a 10-minute soak in hot water, a low-temperature fry to parcook the potatoes, and a high-temperature fry to finish cooking and crisping them. Coating the potato sticks with oil was another key to good browning. The fries often broke when we tossed them in the air-fryer basket, so we moved them to a bowl to toss, resulting in fewer broken pieces. To time the cooking of the potatoes and steak so that both would be ready at the same time, we added the steak to the air fryer partway through cooking the potatoes, placing the meat on the potato sticks. While the cooked steak rested, we crisped the fries, then served our steak frites with parsley-shallot sauce. This recipe can be easily doubled using two steaks (see page 10).

PARSLEY-SHALLOT SAUCE

- ¼ cup minced fresh parsley
- 1 tablespoon extra-virgin olive oil
- 1 tablespoon minced shallot
- 1 tablespoon red wine vinegar
- 1 garlic clove, minced
- ⅛ teaspoon table salt
- Pinch red pepper flakes

STEAK AND FRIES

- 1 pound russet potatoes, peeled
- 5 teaspoons extra-virgin olive oil, divided
- 1 (8- to 12-ounce) top sirloin steak, 1½ inches thick, trimmed
- ½ teaspoon table salt, divided
- ¼ teaspoon pepper

1 FOR THE PARSLEY-SHALLOT SAUCE Combine parsley, oil, shallot, vinegar, 1 tablespoon water, garlic, salt, and pepper flakes in bowl; set aside for serving. (Sauce can be refrigerated for up to 2 days; let come to room temperature and whisk to recombine before serving.)

2 FOR THE STEAK AND FRIES Cut potatoes lengthwise into ½-inch-thick planks. Stack 3 or 4 planks and cut into ½-inch-thick sticks; repeat with remaining planks. Submerge potatoes in large bowl of water and rinse to remove excess starch. Drain potatoes and repeat process as needed until water remains clear. Cover potatoes with hot

water and let sit for 10 minutes. Drain potatoes, transfer to paper towel–lined rimmed baking sheet, and thoroughly pat dry.

3 Toss potatoes with 2 teaspoons oil in clean, dry large bowl. Arrange potatoes in even layer in air-fryer basket. Place basket into air fryer, set temperature to 350 degrees, and cook for 8 minutes. Transfer potatoes to now-empty bowl and toss gently to redistribute. Return potatoes to basket; place basket into air fryer; and cook until softened and potatoes have turned from white to blond (potatoes may be spotty brown at tips), 5 to 10 minutes.

4 Pat steak dry with paper towels, rub with 1 teaspoon oil, and sprinkle with ¼ teaspoon salt and pepper. Transfer potatoes to now-empty bowl and toss with remaining 2 teaspoons oil and remaining ¼ teaspoon salt. Return potatoes to basket and place steak on top. Return basket to air fryer; increase temperature to 400 degrees; and cook until steak is lightly browned and registers 120 to 125 degrees (for medium-rare) or 130 to 135 degrees (for medium), 10 to 15 minutes, flipping and rotating steak halfway through cooking. Transfer steak to cutting board, tent with aluminum foil, and let rest while finishing potatoes.

5 Transfer potatoes to now-empty bowl and toss gently to redistribute. Return potatoes to basket; return basket to air fryer; and cook until golden brown and crisp, 5 to 10 minutes. Season with salt and pepper to taste. Slice steak thin and serve with fries and sauce.

Per Serving Cal 570 | Total Fat 27g | Sat Fat 6g | Chol 90mg | Sodium 810mg
Total Carb 43g | Dietary Fiber 3g | Total Sugars 2g | Added Sugars 0g | Protein 39g

FLANK STEAK WITH CORN AND BLACK BEAN SALAD

Serves 2 | Total Time: 35 minutes

Why This Recipe Works For your next taco night, try using the air fryer and these bright Southwestern flavors. For the black bean and corn salad that accompanies our flank steak, we roasted a poblano chile and scallion whites but liked the convenience of canned beans and frozen corn. Instead of cooking the meat separately, we placed it on top of our poblano and scallion whites to cook, which reduced the cooking time. Chipotle chile powder added smokiness to the steak, and a yogurt-lime dressing, scallion greens, and cilantro flavored the corn and black beans. The dressing also became an aromatic sauce for the meat. If fire-roasted corn is unavailable, substitute traditional frozen corn; avoid canned corn here. This recipe can be easily doubled using two steaks (see page 10). Serve with warm tortillas.

¼ cup plain Greek yogurt

1 teaspoon grated lime zest plus 2 tablespoons juice, plus lime wedges for serving

1½ cups frozen fire-roasted corn, thawed

1 (15-ounce) can black beans, rinsed

1 poblano chile, stemmed, halved, and seeded

4 scallions, white parts cut into 2-inch pieces, green parts sliced thin

1 tablespoon extra-virgin olive oil, divided

1 (8- to 12-ounce) flank steak, 1 inch thick, trimmed

½ teaspoon chipotle chile powder

¼ teaspoon table salt

3 tablespoons chopped fresh cilantro

1 Whisk yogurt and lime zest and juice together in large bowl; measure out and reserve 2 tablespoons dressing for serving. Add corn and beans to remaining dressing and toss to combine; set aside.

2 Toss poblano and scallion whites with 2 teaspoons oil in separate bowl. Transfer to air-fryer basket and spread into even layer. Pat steak dry with paper towels, rub with remaining 1 teaspoon oil, and sprinkle with chile powder and salt. Place steak on top of vegetables. Place basket into air fryer and set temperature to 400 degrees. Cook until steak is lightly browned and registers 120 to 125 degrees (for medium-rare) or 130 to 135 degrees (for medium), 8 to 14 minutes, flipping and rotating steak halfway through cooking.

3 Transfer steak to cutting board, tent with aluminum foil, and let rest while finishing salad. Chop poblano and scallion whites coarse and add to corn mixture along with cilantro and scallion greens. Season with salt and pepper to taste. Slice steak thin against grain and serve with salad, reserved dressing, and lime wedges.

Per Serving Cal 510 | Total Fat 19g | Sat Fat 6g | Chol 70mg | Sodium 810mg
Total Carb 49g | Dietary Fiber 8g | Total Sugars 6g | Added Sugars 0g | Protein 36g

DILL-AND-CORIANDER-RUBBED ROASTED PORK CHOP

Serves 1 to 4 | Total Time: 30 minutes

Why This Recipe Works Spices and herbs add intense flavor to food without changing its calorie count, so they are especially useful when you are trying to cook healthy. Here dill, coriander, and cayenne transformed our boneless pork chop. We incorporated a small amount of sugar to boost browning, and since boneless meat can dry out quickly, we added a touch of oil to the rub to seal in juices so that the chop stayed moist and juicy. The homemade rub was fresher and more aromatic than store-bought options and allowed us to make just the right amount as needed. We enjoyed it so much that we were inspired to create two more easy rubs, one that reminded us of a summer barbecue and another based on the delicate, aromatic blend of herbes de Provence. This recipe is written to serve one but can be easily scaled to serve up to four people (see page 10).

DILL AND CORIANDER RUB

- 1 teaspoon dried dill weed
- ½ teaspoon extra-virgin olive oil
- ½ teaspoon ground coriander
- ¼ teaspoon sugar
- ⅛ teaspoon table salt
- ⅛ teaspoon pepper
- Pinch cayenne pepper

PORK

- 1 (4- to 6-ounce) boneless pork chop, ¾ to 1 inch thick, trimmed

1 FOR THE DILL AND CORIANDER RUB Combine all ingredients in small bowl.

2 FOR THE PORK Pat pork chop dry with paper towels. Using sharp knife, cut 2 slits, about 2 inches apart, through fat on edges of chop. Rub chop with spice rub. Place chop in air-fryer basket. Place basket into air fryer and set temperature to 400 degrees. Cook until chop is lightly browned and registers 140 degrees, 10 to 15 minutes, flipping and rotating chop halfway through cooking. Transfer chop to plate, tent with aluminum foil, and let rest for 5 minutes before serving.

BARBECUE-RUBBED ROASTED PORK CHOP

Combine 1 teaspoon chili powder, ½ teaspoon extra-virgin olive oil, ½ teaspoon pepper, ½ teaspoon brown sugar, ⅛ teaspoon table salt, and pinch cayenne pepper in bowl. Substitute barbecue rub for spice rub in step 2.

HERB-RUBBED ROASTED PORK CHOP

Combine ½ teaspoon extra-virgin olive oil, ½ teaspoon dried thyme, ½ teaspoon dried rosemary, ½ teaspoon dried oregano, ½ teaspoon ground fennel, ¼ teaspoon sugar, and ⅛ teaspoon table salt in bowl. Substitute herb rub for spice rub in step 2.

Per Serving Cal 260 | Total Fat 13g | Sat Fat 4g | Chol 85mg | Sodium 360mg
Total Carb 2g | Dietary Fiber 1g | Total Sugars 1g | Added Sugars 1g | Protein 32g

CRISPY PORK CHOPS WITH ROASTED PEACH, BLACKBERRY, AND ARUGULA SALAD

Serves 2 | Total Time: 1 hour

Why This Recipe Works It's summertime and you're hungry. Did you ever think of pairing ripe in-season peaches and blackberries with a delicious breaded pork chop? We did, and the result was sensational. We coated pork chops with bread crumbs before air-frying them. We also used the air fryer to roast peaches till they were tender and juicy. As we've found with coatings for other proteins, toasted panko gave us the most crunch out of any bread crumbs we tested. However, the crumb topping flaked off when we flipped the chops during cooking. To help it stick, we scored the surface of the chops in a crosshatch pattern, creating additional surface area for the coating to cling to. We also cut two slits on the edges of the chops to prevent them from buckling in the hot air. We tossed our roasted peaches with arugula, juicy blackberries, almonds, and basil for a mouthwatering salad that complemented the rich crunch of the chops. Instead of peaches, you can use nectarines or plums. For more information on toasting nuts in the air fryer, see page 12. This recipe can be easily doubled (see page 10).

- 2 tablespoons extra-virgin olive oil, divided
- 1 small shallot, minced
- 1 tablespoon white wine vinegar
- 1 tablespoon honey
- ½ teaspoon table salt, divided

- 2 ripe but firm peaches, halved and pitted
- 1 cup panko bread crumbs
- 1 large egg
- 1 tablespoon all-purpose flour
- 2 (4- to 6-ounce) boneless pork chops, ¾ to 1 inch thick, trimmed

- 3 ounces (3 cups) baby arugula
- 2½ ounces (½ cup) blackberries or raspberries
- ½ cup torn fresh basil, mint, and/or tarragon
- ¼ cup whole almonds, toasted and chopped coarse

1 Whisk 1 tablespoon oil, shallot, vinegar, honey, and ¼ teaspoon salt together in large bowl. Lightly spray base of air-fryer basket with canola oil spray. Arrange peaches cut side up in prepared basket and brush tops with portion of dressing; set aside remaining dressing. Place basket into air fryer and set temperature to 400 degrees. Cook until peaches are tender and spotty brown, 10 to 15 minutes. Transfer peaches to cutting board and let cool while preparing pork chops.

2 Toss panko with remaining 1 tablespoon oil in shallow dish until evenly coated. Microwave, stirring frequently, until light golden brown, 1 to 3 minutes; let cool slightly. Whisk egg, flour, and remaining ¼ teaspoon salt together in second shallow dish.

3 Pat chops dry with paper towels. Using sharp knife, cut 2 slits, about 2 inches apart, through fat on edges of each chop. Cut ¹⁄₁₆-inch-deep slits, spaced ½ inch apart, in

crosshatch pattern on both sides of chops. Working with 1 chop at a time, dredge in egg mixture, letting excess drip off, then coat with panko mixture, pressing gently to adhere.

4 Arrange chops in now-empty basket, spaced evenly apart. Return basket to air fryer and cook until chops are crispy and register 140 degrees, 12 to 18 minutes, flipping and rotating chops halfway through cooking. Transfer chops to plate and let rest while finishing salad.

5 Cut peaches into 1-inch wedges. Add peaches, arugula, blackberries, basil, and almonds to bowl with reserved dressing and toss gently to combine. Season with salt and pepper to taste. Serve chops with salad.

Per Serving Cal 580 | Total Fat 26g | Sat Fat 5g | Chol 130mg | Sodium 720mg
Total Carb 55g | Dietary Fiber 6g | Total Sugars 24g | Added Sugars 8g | Protein 32g

SWEET AND SPICY GLAZED PORK CHOPS WITH SESAME BOK CHOY

Serves 2 | Total Time: 45 minutes

Why This Recipe Works What could be more appetizing than a glazed pork chop? The sheen on the meat tempts you to cut into it right away. But in the air fryer, glazes tend to slide off meat. Since a thick glaze adheres better, the natural pectin in fruit preserves helped us build such a glaze here. We combined pineapple preserves and rice vinegar as its sweet-and-sour components, with toasted sesame oil, ginger, and chili-garlic sauce lending umami and spice. We parcooked the meat and then brushed the glaze onto the pork in two batches to prevent too much from dripping off at one time. The sweet-and-sour pork paired well with baby bok choy, which fit easily in the air fryer. The bulbs turned tender and the leaves became slightly crispy in the air fryer while the pork rested. We tossed the tender vegetable with a dash of toasted sesame oil, giving it a sheen and echoing the flavor of the oil on the meat. If baby bok choy is unavailable, substitute 12 ounces of traditional bok choy, cut into 2-inch pieces. Bok choy can sometimes be sandy within the base of the head; make sure to remove any sand during washing. For a spicier dish, use the greater amount of chili sauce. This recipe can be easily doubled (see page 10).

- 2 (4- to 6-ounce) boneless pork chops, ¾ to 1 inch thick, trimmed
- 2 tablespoons toasted sesame oil, divided
- ¼ teaspoon table salt

- 2 tablespoons pineapple or apricot preserves
- 1 teaspoon unseasoned rice vinegar
- 1 teaspoon grated fresh ginger
- ¼–¾ teaspoon Asian chili-garlic sauce

- 2 heads baby bok choy (4 to 5 ounces each)
- 2 teaspoons soy sauce
- 2 teaspoons sesame seeds, toasted

1 Pat pork chops dry with paper towels. Using sharp knife, cut 2 slits, about 2 inches apart, through fat on edges of each chop. Rub chops with 1 teaspoon oil, then sprinkle with salt. Arrange chops in air-fryer basket, spaced evenly apart. Place basket into air fryer; set temperature to 400 degrees; and cook until chops begin to brown at edges, 8 to 10 minutes.

2 Microwave preserves, vinegar, ginger, and chili-garlic sauce in small bowl until mixture is fluid, about 30 seconds, stirring halfway through microwaving. Flip and rotate chops, then brush with half of glaze. Return basket to air fryer and cook for 5 minutes. Brush chops with remaining glaze; return basket to air fryer; and continue to cook until chops are lightly browned and register 140 degrees, 3 to 5 minutes. Transfer chops to plate, tent with aluminum foil, and let rest while preparing bok choy.

3 Halve bok choy lengthwise, wash thoroughly, and spin dry. Toss bok choy with 2 teaspoons oil in large bowl and arrange in even layer in now-empty basket. Place basket into air fryer; set temperature to 350 degrees; and cook until bok choy is crisp-tender, about 5 minutes. Transfer bok choy to now-empty bowl and toss with soy sauce, sesame seeds, and remaining 1 tablespoon oil. Serve chops with bok choy.

Per Serving Cal 360 | Total Fat 22g | Sat Fat 4.5g | Chol 60mg | Sodium 730mg
Total Carb 16g | Dietary Fiber 2g | Total Sugars 13g | Added Sugars 0g | Protein 23g

ROASTED BONE-IN PORK CHOP WITH SWEET POTATOES AND MAPLE-ROSEMARY SAUCE

Serves 2 | Total Time: 45 minutes

Why This Recipe Works We tried roasting two 6- to 8-ounce bone-in pork chops together in the air fryer but they didn't quite fit. So we chose a single thick-cut 12- to 16-ounce chop to serve two. We needed to cook this chop long enough for the meat to get tender without the exterior drying out. Roasting at 350 degrees gave us juicy meat and great color. Cutting two slits in the sides of the chop prevented it from curling during cooking. We roasted sweet potatoes under the pork and let the fat from the meat drip onto them, adding rich flavor to their sweetness. The potatoes finished cooking while the pork rested and we served the dish with an aromatic maple syrup sauce. This recipe can be easily doubled (see page 10).

1 pound sweet potatoes, unpeeled, halved lengthwise and sliced crosswise ¾ inch thick

1 tablespoon canola oil, divided

½ teaspoon table salt, divided

1 (12- to 16-ounce) bone-in pork rib or center-cut chop, 1 to 1½ inches thick, trimmed

¼ teaspoon pepper

3 tablespoons maple syrup

2 teaspoons cider vinegar

½ teaspoon minced fresh rosemary

¼ teaspoon cornstarch

Pinch cayenne pepper

Pinch ground cloves

1 Toss potatoes with 2 teaspoons oil and ¼ teaspoon salt in bowl and arrange in even layer in air-fryer basket. Place basket into air fryer, set temperature to 350 degrees, and cook for 10 minutes.

2 Pat pork chop dry with paper towels. Using sharp knife, cut 2 slits, about 2 inches apart, through fat on edges of chop. Rub chop with remaining 1 teaspoon oil, then sprinkle with pepper and remaining ¼ teaspoon salt. Place chop on top of potatoes. Return basket to air fryer and cook until chop is lightly browned and registers 140 degrees, 15 to 20 minutes, flipping and rotating chop halfway through cooking.

3 Transfer chop to cutting board, tent with aluminum foil, and let rest while finishing potatoes and sauce. Return basket to air-fryer and cook until potatoes are browned and tender, 3 to 5 minutes.

4 Whisk maple syrup, vinegar, rosemary, cornstarch, cayenne, and cloves together in small bowl. Microwave until thickened, about 30 seconds, stirring halfway through microwaving. Season with salt and pepper to taste. Carve pork from bone and slice ½ inch thick. Serve pork with potatoes and sauce.

Per Serving Cal 610 | Total Fat 21g | Sat Fat 5g | Chol 105mg | Sodium 780mg
Total Carb 66g | Dietary Fiber 7g | Total Sugars 28g | Added Sugars 18g | Protein 36g

LEMON-THYME PORK TENDERLOIN WITH GREEN BEANS AND HAZELNUTS

Serves 2 | Total Time: 45 minutes

Why This Recipe Works Mild, buttery pork tenderloin is a great choice for a weeknight because it cooks quickly, easily takes on the flavor of an herb or spice rub, and makes a complete meal when accompanied by a healthy side—here we use green beans and hazelnuts. We easily fit the tenderloin in the air fryer by cutting it in half crosswise. A concentrated paste of honey, mustard, thyme, and lemon zest flavored the pork and helped it brown, and a relatively low roasting temperature ensured that the meat cooked evenly and didn't dry out. Lemon and thyme made a second appearance, dressing the cooked green beans to punch up the flavor, while roasted red peppers, fresh parsley, and crunchy toasted hazelnuts rounded out the side dish for the pork. For more information on toasting nuts in the air fryer, see page 12. This recipe can be easily doubled (see page 10).

- 1 pound green beans, trimmed
- 2 tablespoons extra-virgin olive oil, divided
- ⅜ teaspoon table salt, divided
- ¼ teaspoon pepper, divided

- 2 teaspoons grated lemon zest, divided, plus 1 tablespoon juice
- 1½ teaspoons minced fresh thyme, divided
- 1 small garlic clove, minced to paste
- 1 teaspoon Dijon mustard
- 1 teaspoon honey

- 1 (12-ounce) pork tenderloin, trimmed and halved crosswise
- ½ cup jarred roasted red peppers, rinsed, patted dry, and sliced thin
- ¼ cup chopped fresh parsley
- ¼ cup hazelnuts or almonds, toasted, skinned, and chopped

1 Toss green beans with 1 tablespoon oil, ⅛ teaspoon salt, and ⅛ teaspoon pepper in large bowl. Arrange green beans in even layer in air-fryer basket. Combine 2 teaspoons oil, 1 teaspoon lemon zest, lemon juice, ½ teaspoon thyme, and garlic in now-empty bowl; set aside.

2 Combine mustard, honey, remaining 1 teaspoon oil, remaining ¼ teaspoon salt, remaining ⅛ teaspoon pepper, remaining 1 teaspoon lemon zest, and remaining 1 teaspoon thyme in separate bowl. Pat pork dry with paper towels, then rub with mustard mixture. Arrange pork on top of green beans, spaced evenly apart. (Tuck thinner tail end of tenderloin under itself as needed to create uniform pieces.) Place basket into air fryer and set temperature to 350 degrees. Cook until green beans are tender and pork is lightly browned and registers 140 degrees, 18 to 24 minutes, flipping and rotating pork halfway through cooking.

3 Transfer pork to cutting board, tent with aluminum foil, and let rest for 5 minutes. Add green beans, red peppers, parsley, and hazelnuts to bowl with dressing and toss to combine. Season with salt and pepper to taste. Slice pork thin and serve with green bean mixture.

Per Serving Cal 490 | Total Fat 27g | Sat Fat 4g | Chol 105mg | Sodium 770mg
Total Carb 23g | Dietary Fiber 7g | Total Sugars 12g | Added Sugars 3g | Protein 40g

MARINATED PORK GYROS

Serves 2 | Total Time: 45 minutes

Why This Recipe Works Though the pork for these wraps is not made on the traditional spit used for gyros, the air fryer's high heat on the exterior of the meat helps it cook in a similar fashion to its inspiration. We opted to use country-style pork ribs, which are meatier than pork chops. They take a bit longer to cook than pork chops, allowing more time to develop color and crispy, tasty char. Before cooking, we coated the ribs in a flavorful marinade of garlic, oregano, coriander, and paprika, reserving half of it to use once the pork was cooked. While the pork roasted, we assembled a quick tzatziki (a Greek yogurt, cucumber, and garlic sauce). Persian, aka "mini," cucumbers were perfectly suited here. Rather than peel and seed half an English cucumber, all we had to do was shred one Persian cucumber, seeds and all, and slice a second one thin as a topping. Other toppings included a shallot and baby kale. Any baby green you have on hand would work fine, too. Remember the remaining marinade? We turned it into a dressing by whisking in some lemon juice. After slicing the pork thin, we tossed the meat with the dressing before assembling the gyros, making sure that every inch of the meat was coated in spiced, garlicky goodness. Use half an English cucumber if you can't find Persian ones. This recipe can be easily doubled (see page 10).

- 1 tablespoon extra-virgin olive oil
- 3 garlic cloves, minced, divided
- 1 teaspoon dried oregano
- 1 teaspoon ground coriander
- 1 teaspoon paprika
- ½ teaspoon table salt, divided
- ½ teaspoon pepper, divided
- 8 ounces boneless country-style pork ribs, trimmed
- 2 Persian cucumbers, divided
- 6 tablespoons plain Greek yogurt
- 1 tablespoon lemon juice, divided, plus lemon wedges for serving
- 1 teaspoon minced fresh dill
- 2 (8-inch) pitas
- 1 cup baby kale or spinach
- 1 shallot, halved and sliced thin

1 Microwave oil, two-thirds garlic, oregano, coriander, paprika, ¼ teaspoon salt, and ¼ teaspoon pepper in medium bowl until fragrant, about 30 seconds.

2 Rub ribs with half of oil mixture, then arrange in air-fryer basket, spaced evenly apart. Place basket into air fryer and set temperature to 400 degrees. Cook until ribs are lightly browned and register 150 degrees, 6 to 10 minutes, flipping ribs halfway through cooking. Transfer ribs to cutting board, tent with aluminum foil, and let rest for 5 minutes.

3 Shred 1 cucumber to yield ¼ cup; slice remaining cucumber thin. Combine shredded cucumber, yogurt, 1 teaspoon lemon juice, dill, remaining garlic, remaining ¼ teaspoon salt, and remaining ¼ teaspoon pepper in separate bowl. Season with salt and pepper to taste.

4 Stack pitas and wrap tightly with foil. Place pita packet in now-empty basket. Return basket to air fryer and cook until pitas are heated through, 2 to 4 minutes. Whisk remaining 2 teaspoons lemon juice into remaining oil mixture. Slice pork thin and toss with lemon-oil mixture. Divide pork evenly among pitas and top with tzatziki, sliced cucumber, kale, and shallot. Serve with lemon wedges.

Per Serving Cal 510 | Total Fat 21g | Sat Fat 7g | Chol 95mg | Sodium 930mg
Total Carb 44g | Dietary Fiber 3g | Total Sugars 4g | Added Sugars 0g | Protein 37g

SEAFOOD

96 Pistachio-Crusted Salmon
   Hazelnut-Crusted Salmon
   Smoked Almond–Crusted Salmon

98 Honey-Glazed Salmon with
   Snap Peas and Radishes

101 Sesame Salmon with Roasted
   Kimchi, Broccoli, and Shiitakes

102 Salmon Burgers with Tomato Chutney

105 Harissa-Rubbed Haddock with
   Brussels Sprouts and Leek

106 Crispy Halibut with Leafy Greens
   and Tartar Sauce

108 Roasted Swordfish with Asparagus
   and Citrus Salad

110 Ginger-Turmeric Scallops with
   Mango and Cucumber Salad

112 Spicy Roasted Shrimp and
   Fennel Salad with Cannellini Beans
   and Watercress

114 Shrimp with Curry Noodles

117 Chipotle Shrimp Tacos

PISTACHIO-CRUSTED SALMON

Serves 1 to 4 | Total Time: 30 minutes

Why This Recipe Works What could be better than a nice piece of salmon for someone who wants to eat healthy and still enjoy rich flavor? Luckily, the circulating high heat of the air fryer cooks seafood quickly, keeping it tender and retaining its nutrients. We often enhance the flavor and texture of fish with spices or crunchy nut crusts. For this recipe, we placed the nut crust on only the top of the fillet so that the fish didn't need to be turned during air-frying and the crust couldn't get soggy on the bottom. Thick Greek yogurt helped the nuts stick to the fish. We used healthy pistachios here (and hazelnuts and smoked almonds for the variations) and found that chopping them fine (with a knife, spice grinder, or mini food processor) was essential for an even coating. Panko bread crumbs fortified the crust, and patting the salmon dry helped the crust stay on. A foil sling set in the air-fryer basket allowed us to deftly pick up the cooked fish without breakage. We often use oil spray on the foil sling when cooking delicate fish fillets; here the skin adheres to the foil in case you want to remove it. Simply slide a spatula under the fillet and leave the skin behind. If using wild salmon, cook it until it registers 120 degrees. For more information on using a foil sling in your air fryer, see page 5. This recipe is written to serve one but can be easily scaled to serve up to four people (see page 10).

1 tablespoon finely chopped toasted pistachios or almonds

1 tablespoon panko bread crumbs

1 tablespoon minced fresh parsley

¼ teaspoon fennel seeds, chopped

1 (4- to 6-ounce) skin-on salmon fillet, 1 to 1½ inches thick

⅛ teaspoon table salt

2 teaspoons plain Greek yogurt

Olive oil spray

1 Make sling for air-fryer basket by folding 1 long sheet of aluminum foil so it is 4 inches wide. Lay sheet of foil widthwise across basket, pressing foil into and up sides of basket. Fold excess foil as needed so edges of foil are flush with top of basket.

2 Combine pistachios, panko, parsley, and fennel seeds in shallow dish. Pat salmon dry with paper towels and sprinkle with salt. Spread yogurt evenly on flesh side of salmon, then dredge coated side in pistachio mixture, pressing gently to adhere.

3 Arrange salmon, skin side down, on prepared sling and lightly spray top with oil spray. (Space additional fillets evenly apart.) Place basket into air fryer and set temperature to 400 degrees. Cook until salmon is lightly browned and center is still translucent when checked with tip of paring knife and registers 125 degrees (for medium-rare), 8 to 10 minutes.

4 Using sling, carefully remove salmon from air fryer. Slide fish spatula along underside of salmon and transfer to plate, leaving skin behind. Serve.

HAZELNUT-CRUSTED SALMON
Substitute hazelnuts or pecans for pistachios, ½ teaspoon minced fresh oregano for parsley, and ½ teaspoon grated lemon zest for fennel seeds.

SMOKED ALMOND–CRUSTED SALMON
Substitute smoked almonds or smoked peanuts for pistachios, chives for parsley, and ¼ teaspoon paprika and pinch cayenne pepper for fennel seeds.

Per Serving Cal 320 | Total Fat 20g | Sat Fat 5g | Chol 65mg | Sodium 370mg
Total Carb 7g | Dietary Fiber 1g | Total Sugars 1g | Added Sugars 0g | Protein 26g

HONEY-GLAZED SALMON WITH SNAP PEAS AND RADISHES

Serves 2 | Total Time: 35 minutes

Why This Recipe Works A glaze coats, flavors, and protects fish from drying out during air-frying. For this glaze, we combined honey; soy sauce; and tahini (sesame paste), which added nuttiness and helped the mixture cling better to the fish. The air fryer's direct heat caramelized the glaze's sugars from above while the circulated air cooked our salmon from all sides. We brushed the glaze on the fish once before cooking and then again halfway through. After about 8 minutes, our glazed fish had browned edges and a tender interior. While the salmon rested, we roasted fresh snap peas and radishes until they were crisp-tender so that they retained their green and pink hues and complemented the orange salmon beautifully for a vivid and appetizing plate. If using wild salmon, cook it until it registers 120 degrees. For more information on using a foil sling in your air fryer, see page 5. This recipe can be easily doubled (see page 10).

- 2 tablespoons honey
- 1 tablespoon tahini
- 1 tablespoon soy sauce
- 1 teaspoon lime juice, plus lime wedges for serving

- 2 (4- to 6-ounce) skin-on salmon fillets, 1 to 1½ inches thick
- 8 ounces sugar snap peas, strings removed
- 8 radishes, trimmed and quartered

- 1 teaspoon toasted sesame oil
- ⅛ teaspoon table salt
- 2 scallions, sliced thin
- 1 tablespoon sesame seeds, toasted

1 Make sling for air-fryer basket by folding 1 long sheet of aluminum foil so it is 4 inches wide. Lay sheet of foil widthwise across basket, pressing foil into and up sides of basket. Fold excess foil as needed so edges of foil are flush with top of basket.

2 Whisk honey, tahini, soy sauce, and lime juice together in bowl. Measure out 2 tablespoons glaze for cooking; set aside remaining glaze for serving. Pat salmon dry with paper towels. Brush flesh side of salmon with 1 tablespoon glaze for cooking. Arrange salmon, skin side down, on prepared sling. Place basket into air fryer, set temperature to 400 degrees, and cook for 5 minutes.

3 Brush salmon with remaining 1 tablespoon glaze for cooking. Return basket to air fryer and cook until salmon is well browned and center is still translucent when checked with tip of paring knife and registers 125 degrees (for medium-rare), 3 to 5 minutes.

4 Using sling, carefully remove salmon from air fryer. Slide fish spatula along underside of salmon and transfer to serving platter, leaving skin behind. Tent with foil and let rest while preparing peas and radishes.

5 Toss peas and radishes with oil and salt in bowl and arrange in even layer in now-empty basket. Return basket to air fryer and cook until crisp-tender, about 5 minutes. Transfer vegetables to platter with salmon and sprinkle salmon with scallions and sesame seeds. Serve with lime wedges and reserved glaze.

Per Serving Cal 330 | Total Fat 16g | Sat Fat 3g | Chol 30mg | Sodium 660mg
Total Carb 30g | Dietary Fiber 5g | Total Sugars 21g | Added Sugars 16g | Protein 18g

SESAME SALMON WITH ROASTED KIMCHI, BROCCOLI, AND SHIITAKES

Serves 2 | Total Time: 35 minutes

Why This Recipe Works We paired spicy cabbage kimchi, a popular Korean condiment, with salmon for this piquant and satisfying one-pan supper. Pan? An air fryer's wire basket doesn't allow for cooking with juicy ingredients like kimchi so we placed chopped kimchi, broccoli, and shiitake mushrooms—tossed with fresh ginger, mirin, soy sauce, and sesame oil—in a small cake pan and set that in the basket to cook. Flavorful liquid didn't drip away into the base but collected in the bottom of the pan instead and kept our ingredients moist. Once the vegetables were softened and lightly browned, we placed salmon pieces topped with toasted sesame seeds on them to air-fry. The tartness and gentle heat of the pickled cabbage made a flavorful contrast to the rich sesame-crusted fish. If using wild salmon, cook it until it registers 120 degrees. You will need a 6-inch round nonstick or silicone cake pan for this recipe; before starting this recipe, confirm your air fryer allows enough space for the pan.

- 1 cup cabbage kimchi, drained and cut into 1-inch pieces
- 3 ounces 1-inch broccoli florets (1 cup)
- 4 ounces shiitake mushrooms, stemmed and sliced thin
- 1 tablespoon mirin
- 2 teaspoons grated fresh ginger
- 1 teaspoon soy sauce
- 1 teaspoon toasted sesame oil, plus extra for drizzling
- 1 (8- to 12-ounce) skinless salmon fillet, 1-1½ inches thick, cut into 2-inch pieces
- 1 tablespoon sesame seeds, toasted
- 1 scallion, sliced thin

1 Combine kimchi, broccoli, mushrooms, mirin, ginger, soy sauce, and oil in bowl. Transfer kimchi mixture to 6-inch round nonstick or silicone cake pan and spread into even layer. Place pan in air-fryer basket and place basket into air fryer. Set temperature to 400 degrees and cook until vegetables are softened and lightly browned, 8 to 14 minutes, stirring halfway through cooking.

2 Pat salmon pieces dry with paper towels and sprinkle tops with sesame seeds, pressing gently to adhere. Arrange salmon on top of kimchi mixture. Return basket to air fryer and cook until salmon is lightly browned and center is still translucent when checked with tip of paring knife and registers 125 degrees (for medium-rare), 8 to 10 minutes. Remove pan from air fryer. Sprinkle salmon with scallion and drizzle with extra oil. Serve.

Per Serving Cal 350 | Total Fat 21g | Sat Fat 4g | Chol 60mg | Sodium 620mg
Total Carb 11g | Dietary Fiber 3g | Total Sugars 5g | Added Sugars 0g | Protein 28g

SALMON BURGERS WITH TOMATO CHUTNEY

Serves 2 | Total Time: 45 minutes

Why This Recipe Works Since salmon prepared in the air fryer consistently turns out well cooked and moist, we tried using the meaty, nutritious fish to make tender burgers. We paired them with a quick, sweet-tangy tomato chutney that is easily made in the microwave. Since the chutney uses pantry ingredients (brown sugar, cider vinegar, and canned tomatoes), you can make it any time and use it instead of ketchup. For our quick-cooking burgers, we preferred to chop the salmon in the food processor for a textured combination of finely minced and coarsely chopped pieces. We bound the patties with crunchy panko (and a little yogurt) so that they held their shape but weren't mushy. We gave the patties some freshness by combining the panko-salmon mixture with cilantro, lemon juice, and scallion whites. The chutney can be made up to three days in advance, making burger night easier. If using wild salmon, cook the burgers until they register 120 degrees. This recipe can be easily doubled (see page 10).

- ¾ cup canned diced tomatoes, drained and patted dry
- 1 tablespoon packed light brown sugar
- 2 teaspoons cider vinegar
- ¼ teaspoon table salt, divided

- ¼ teaspoon pepper, divided
- 2 scallions, white and green parts separated and sliced thin
- ¼ cup chopped fresh cilantro, divided
- 12 ounces skinless salmon fillets, cut into 1-inch pieces

- 3 tablespoons panko bread crumbs
- 1 tablespoon plain yogurt
- 2 teaspoons lemon juice
- 2 hamburger buns, toasted if desired
- 2 leaves Bibb lettuce

1 Microwave tomatoes, sugar, vinegar, ⅛ teaspoon salt, and ⅛ teaspoon pepper in bowl until mixture is thickened, about 8 minutes, stirring halfway through microwaving. Let chutney cool completely, then stir in scallion greens and 1 tablespoon cilantro. Season with salt and pepper to taste; set aside for serving. (Chutney can be refrigerated for up to 3 days.)

2 Pulse salmon in food processor until there is even mix of finely minced and coarsely chopped pieces, about 2 pulses, scraping down sides of bowl as needed. Stir panko,

yogurt, lemon juice, scallion whites, remaining ⅛ teaspoon salt, remaining ⅛ teaspoon pepper, and remaining 3 tablespoons cilantro together in large bowl. Fold in salmon gently until just combined.

3 Lightly spray base of air-fryer basket with canola oil spray. Using your lightly moistened hands, divide salmon mixture in half, shape into 2 lightly packed balls, and flatten each ball gently into 1-inch-thick patty. Press center of each patty with your fingertips to create ¼-inch-deep depression.

4 Arrange patties in prepared basket, spaced evenly apart. Place basket into air fryer and set temperature to 350 degrees. Cook until burgers are lightly browned and centers are still translucent when checked with tip of paring knife and register 125 degrees (for medium-rare), 6 to 8 minutes, flipping burgers halfway through cooking.

If desired, arrange bun tops and bottoms cut side up in now-empty basket. Return basket to air fryer, set temperature to 400, and cook until buns are lightly toasted, 4 to 6 minutes. Serve burgers on buns, topped with chutney and lettuce.

Per Serving Cal 570 | Total Fat 25g | Sat Fat 6g | Chol 95mg | Sodium 840mg
Total Carb 41g | Dietary Fiber 2g | Total Sugars 13g | Added Sugars 7g | Protein 41g

HARISSA-RUBBED HADDOCK WITH BRUSSELS SPROUTS AND LEEK

Serves 2 | Total Time: 35 minutes

Why This Recipe Works For this beautifully satisfying dinner that's great for a date night, we air-fried a hearty pile of vegetables—earthy brussels sprouts and a tender leek—with halibut. We used harissa, a North African spice paste, to create a zesty crust on the mild-flavored fish. The vegetables got a head start so that they could begin to soften, and then they finished cooking underneath the fish at a hotter temperature to crisp up and char around the edges. Cutting the leek into large pieces, 1-inch thick, helped it cook alongside the hardier sprouts without getting overly charred. Look for small brussels sprouts no bigger than a golf ball, as they're likely to be sweeter and more tender than large sprouts. If you can find only large sprouts, quarter them. Black sea bass, cod, hake, and pollack are good substitutes for the haddock. Tail-end fillets can be folded to achieve the proper thickness. This recipe can be easily doubled (see page 10).

12 ounces brussels sprouts, trimmed and halved	3 tablespoons extra-virgin olive oil, divided	2 (4- to 6-ounce) skinless haddock fillets, 1 to 1½ inches thick
1 large leek, white and light green parts only, halved lengthwise, sliced 1 inch thick, and washed thoroughly	½ teaspoon table salt, divided 4 teaspoons harissa paste	1 teaspoon grated lemon zest, plus lemon wedges for serving

1 Toss brussels sprouts and leek with 2 tablespoons oil and ¼ teaspoon salt in bowl. Arrange vegetables in even layer in air-fryer basket. Place basket into air fryer; set temperature to 350 degrees; and cook for 10 minutes, stirring vegetables halfway through cooking.

2 Combine harissa paste, remaining 1 tablespoon oil, and remaining ¼ teaspoon salt in small bowl. Pat haddock dry with paper towels and rub with harissa mixture. Stir vegetables, then place fillets, skinned side down, on top,

spaced evenly apart. Return basket to air fryer; increase temperature to 400 degrees; and cook until haddock is lightly browned, flakes apart when prodded gently with paring knife, and registers 135 degrees, 8 to 14 minutes.

3 Transfer haddock to serving platter. Stir lemon zest into vegetables and season with salt and pepper to taste. Transfer vegetables to platter with haddock and serve with lemon wedges.

Per Serving Cal 330 | Total Fat 22g | Sat Fat 3g | Chol 30mg | Sodium 830mg
Total Carb 21g | Dietary Fiber 7g | Total Sugars 6g | Added Sugars 0g | Protein 15g

CRISPY HALIBUT WITH LEAFY GREENS AND TARTAR SAUCE

Serves 2 | Total Time: 45 minutes

Why This Recipe Works There's no denying the appeal of a plate of fried fish, so we wanted to create a flavorful and healthy version without the deep frying. We air-fried breaded fish and added a salad instead of french fries for a stunning, light, and summery plate. We toasted panko bread crumbs in the microwave and then mixed in fresh parsley and lemon zest. After brushing one side of the halibut with yogurt, we coated that side with the toasted panko and air-fried the fish until it was moist and tender. While flaky white fish should be cooked to 135 degrees, we cook meatier fish (such as halibut) to 130 degrees and then let it rise in temperature while it rests. This prevents moisture loss from high-heat cooking. Instead of a heavy mayonnaise-based tartar sauce to pair with the halibut, we created one with yogurt, chopped pickles, pickle brine, and lemon juice. We got a second use out of the sauce by also using it to dress our simple salad of buttery Bibb lettuce and cherry tomatoes. Mahi-mahi, red snapper, striped bass, and swordfish are good substitutes for the halibut. Tail-end fillets can be folded to achieve the proper thickness. For more information on using a foil sling in your air fryer, see page 5. This recipe can be easily doubled (see page 10).

5 tablespoons plain Greek yogurt, divided

¼ cup minced fresh parsley, tarragon, and/or dill, divided

2 tablespoons finely chopped dill pickles plus 1 teaspoon brine

4 teaspoons extra-virgin olive oil, divided

1 small shallot, minced

½ teaspoon grated lemon zest plus 1 tablespoon juice

⅛ teaspoon pepper

⅓ cup panko bread crumbs

2 (4- to 6-ounce) skinless halibut fillets, 1 to 1½ inches thick

¼ teaspoon table salt

½ head Bibb lettuce (4 ounces), torn into bite-size pieces

4 ounces cherry tomatoes, halved

1 Whisk ¼ cup yogurt, 3 tablespoons parsley, pickles and brine, 1 tablespoon oil, shallot, lemon juice, and pepper together in bowl. Season with salt and pepper to taste; set aside tartar sauce for serving.

2 Make sling for air-fryer basket by folding 1 long sheet of aluminum foil so it is 4 inches wide. Lay sheet of foil width-wise across basket, pressing foil into and up sides of basket. Fold excess foil as needed so edges of foil are flush with top of basket. Lightly spray foil with canola oil spray.

3 Toss panko with remaining 1 teaspoon oil in shallow dish until evenly coated. Microwave, stirring frequently, until light golden brown, 1 to 3 minutes. Let cool slightly, then stir in lemon zest and remaining 1 tablespoon parsley. Pat halibut dry with paper towels and sprinkle with salt. Spread remaining 1 tablespoon yogurt evenly on flesh side of halibut, then dredge coated side in panko mixture, pressing gently to adhere.

4 Arrange fillets, skinned side down, on prepared sling, spaced evenly apart. Place basket into air fryer and set temperature to 400 degrees. Cook until halibut is lightly browned, flakes apart when prodded gently with paring knife, and registers 130 degrees, 5 to 10 minutes. Using sling, carefully remove halibut from air fryer. Transfer to individual plates and let rest while preparing salad.

5 Toss lettuce and tomatoes with 2 tablespoons tartar sauce in medium bowl and season with salt and pepper to taste. Serve halibut with salad, passing remaining tartar sauce separately.

Per Serving Cal 320 | Total Fat 15g | Sat Fat 5g | Chol 65mg | Sodium 490mg
Total Carb 19g | Dietary Fiber 2g | Total Sugars 5g | Added Sugars 0g | Protein 27g

ROASTED SWORDFISH WITH ASPARAGUS AND CITRUS SALAD

Serves 2 | Total Time: 45 minutes

Why This Recipe Works The speed and convenience of the air fryer make it great for everyday use, but it is also perfect for special occasions and special ingredients, such as swordfish. Difficult to fish and in high demand for its rich, meaty flesh, swordfish is expensive—definitely worth cooking on red-letter days. The air fryer turned out to be a perfect match because the quick cooking preserved the delicate texture and flavor of the fish and kept its nutrients intact. We knew from previous non–air fryer testing that slow-cooking swordfish gives its enzymes too much time to break it down, rendering it mushy. So the evenly distributed high heat surrounding the swordfish in the air fryer worked in our favor, quickly yielding a superbly tender, juicy interior and a delicately bronzed exterior. A vibrant salad of roasted asparagus and scallions tossed with juicy grapefruit and orange was a fresh and elegant accompaniment for the fish. A sprinkling of dukkah—a fragrant Egyptian condiment made from spices, seeds, and nuts—gave the dish a light finishing crunch. Halibut, mahi-mahi, red snapper, and striped bass are good substitutes for the swordfish. Depending on the size of your air fryer, you may need to halve the asparagus and scallions crosswise to get them to fit. This recipe can be easily doubled (see page 10).

- 12 ounces asparagus, trimmed
- 6 scallions, trimmed
- 2 tablespoons extra-virgin olive oil, divided
- ½ teaspoon table salt, divided
- ¼ teaspoon pepper, divided
- 2 (4- to 6-ounce) skinless swordfish steaks, 1 to 1½ inches thick
- 1 red grapefruit
- 1 orange, plus 2 teaspoons grated orange zest
- ½ cup torn fresh mint, basil, parsley, and/or tarragon
- 2 tablespoons dukkah

1 Toss asparagus and scallions with 1 teaspoon oil, ¼ teaspoon salt, and ⅛ teaspoon pepper in bowl. Arrange vegetables in even layer in air-fryer basket. Place basket into air fryer; set temperature to 400 degrees; and cook until vegetables are tender and lightly charred, about 5 minutes, tossing halfway through cooking. Transfer vegetables to cutting board and let cool while preparing swordfish.

2 Pat swordfish dry with paper towels. Brush with 1 teaspoon oil and sprinkle with remaining ¼ teaspoon salt and remaining ⅛ teaspoon pepper. Arrange swordfish steaks in now-empty basket, spaced evenly apart. Return basket to air fryer and cook until swordfish is lightly browned, flakes apart when prodded gently with paring knife, and registers 130 degrees, 8 to 14 minutes, flipping steaks halfway through cooking. Let swordfish rest while finishing salad.

3 Cut away peel and pith from grapefruit and orange. Cut each citrus fruit from pole to pole into 8 wedges, then cut wedges crosswise into ½-inch-thick pieces. Add citrus pieces to large bowl. Cut asparagus into 2-inch lengths and cut scallions into ½-inch pieces.

Add vegetables, mint, orange zest, and remaining 4 teaspoons oil to bowl with citrus and toss gently to combine. Season with salt and pepper to taste. Serve swordfish with asparagus and citrus salad, sprinkling individual portions with dukkah.

Per Serving Cal 460 | Total Fat 25g | Sat Fat 4.5g | Chol 75mg | Sodium 680mg
Total Carb 33g | Dietary Fiber 12g | Total Sugars 19g | Added Sugars 0g | Protein 28g

GINGER-TURMERIC SCALLOPS WITH MANGO AND CUCUMBER SALAD

Serves 2 | Total Time: 30 minutes

Why This Recipe Works We love scallops, but they need close attention while they cook in a skillet to prevent them from getting tough and rubbery. So we air-fried them and ended up with sea scallops that were sweet and succulent on the inside and delicately browned on the outside. To complement the scallops' sweetness, we made a mango and cucumber salad and flavored some olive oil with a heady blend of fresh ginger, turmeric, and coriander. We used some of the oil to coat the scallops, which gave them a gorgeous golden hue and delicious flavor, and combined the rest with shallot, Thai chile, and lime zest and juice for a spicy salad dressing. If a Thai chile is unavailable, you can substitute a small jalapeño. We recommend buying "dry" scallops, which don't have chemical additives and taste better than "wet." Dry scallops will look ivory or pinkish; wet scallops are bright white. This recipe can be easily doubled (see page 10).

12 ounces large sea scallops, tendons removed

5 teaspoons extra-virgin olive oil

2 teaspoons grated fresh ginger

1 teaspoon honey

½ teaspoon ground turmeric

½ teaspoon ground coriander

¼ teaspoon table salt

1 teaspoon grated lime zest plus 1 tablespoon juice, plus lime wedges for serving

1 shallot, sliced thin

1 Thai chile, stemmed and sliced thin

1 English cucumber, shaved lengthwise into ribbons

1 mango, peeled, pitted, and sliced thin

¼ cup fresh cilantro leaves

2 tablespoons roasted pepitas

1 Place scallops on rimmed baking sheet lined with clean dish towel. Place second clean dish towel on top of scallops and press gently on towel to blot liquid. Let scallops sit at room temperature, covered with towel, for 10 minutes.

2 Whisk oil, ginger, honey, turmeric, coriander, and salt together in small bowl. Microwave until fragrant, about 30 seconds; let cool slightly. Whisk 1 tablespoon oil mixture and lime zest and juice together in large bowl. Stir in shallot and Thai chile and set aside.

3 Toss scallops with remaining oil mixture in separate bowl. Arrange scallops in air-fryer basket, spaced evenly apart. Place basket into air fryer and set temperature to 400 degrees. Cook until scallops are firm to touch and spotty brown, 6 to 10 minutes, flipping scallops halfway through cooking.

4 Add cucumber, mango, cilantro, and pepitas to bowl with dressing and toss gently to combine. Season with salt and pepper to taste. Divide salad between individual serving plates and top with scallops. Serve with lime wedges.

Per Serving Cal 420 | Total Fat 17g | Sat Fat 2.5g | Chol 40mg | Sodium 960mg
Total Carb 42g | Dietary Fiber 6g | Total Sugars 28g | Added Sugars 3g | Protein 26g

SPICY ROASTED SHRIMP AND FENNEL SALAD WITH CANNELLINI BEANS AND WATERCRESS

Serves 2 | Total Time: 45 minutes

Why This Recipe Works This sumptuous main course salad bursting with spice, sweetness, and color brings together an unlikely combination of ingredients. But why do we use the air fryer for a quick-cooking protein like shrimp? It makes the process hands-off and easy. We tossed fennel and shrimp in a spicy, sharp mixture of extra-virgin olive oil, tart tomato paste, oregano, pepper flakes, and fresh garlic. Then we softened and lightly browned the fennel. Now it was just a matter of placing our shrimp on the vegetable and cooking them till they were tender. We used the remaining oil mixture to toss the fennel and shrimp with cannellini beans, sun-dried tomatoes, watercress, and pepperoncini. Large shrimp (26 to 30 per pound) will also work here; adjust the cooking time as needed. If your fennel doesn't have fronds, omit them. For a spicier dish, use the larger amount of pepper flakes. This recipe can be easily doubled (see page 10).

- 3 tablespoons extra-virgin olive oil
- 1 tablespoon tomato paste
- 2 garlic cloves, minced
- ¼ teaspoon dried oregano
- ¼–½ teaspoon red pepper flakes

- 1 large fennel bulb (1 pound), fronds minced, stalks discarded, bulb halved, cored, and sliced thin
- 12 ounces extra-large shrimp (21 to 25 per pound), peeled, deveined, and tails removed
- 1 (15-ounce) can cannellini beans, rinsed

- 2 ounces (2 cups) watercress, cut into 2-inch lengths
- 2 tablespoons oil-packed sun-dried tomatoes, rinsed, patted dry, and chopped
- 2 tablespoons sliced pepperoncini plus 1 tablespoon brine

1 Whisk oil, tomato paste, garlic, oregano, and pepper flakes together in large bowl. Microwave until fragrant, about 30 seconds.

2 Toss sliced fennel with 1 teaspoon oil mixture in separate bowl. Arrange fennel in even layer in air-fryer basket. Place basket into air fryer and set temperature to 400 degrees. Cook until fennel is softened and lightly browned at the edges, 10 to 15 minutes, tossing halfway through cooking.

3 Toss shrimp with 1 teaspoon oil mixture in now-empty bowl. Arrange shrimp in even layer on top of fennel. Return basket to air fryer and cook until shrimp are opaque throughout, 6 to 8 minutes, flipping shrimp halfway through cooking.

4 Add fennel and shrimp mixture, beans, watercress, tomatoes, pepperoncini and brine, and fennel fronds to remaining oil mixture and toss gently to combine. Season with salt and pepper to taste. Serve.

Per Serving Cal 470 | Total Fat 24g | Sat Fat 3.5g | Chol 145mg | Sodium 1060mg
Total Carb 40g | Dietary Fiber 12g | Total Sugars 10g | Added Sugars 0g | Protein 27g

SHRIMP WITH CURRY NOODLES

Serves 2 | Total Time: 45 minutes

Why This Recipe Works The inspiration for this recipe was Singapore noodles, an iconic dish from Hong Kong. We soaked rice vermicelli in boiling water and used the air fryer to cook the shrimp, carrot, and bell pepper. These were all flavored with curry powder, the traditional spice blend used for the dish. We started by blooming the curry powder and other aromatics in oil, which smoothed out the texture and intensified the flavor. We tossed the vegetables in some of the aromatic oil and air-fried them until they softened. Then we tossed halved shrimp with the curry powder–infused oil before air-frying them on top of the vegetables so that both finished cooking at the same time. Finally, we mixed the shrimp and vegetables, crunchy bean sprouts, cilantro, and scallions with the noodles for a delightfully spicy meal. Large shrimp (26 to 30 per pound) will also work here; adjust the cooking time as needed. This recipe can be easily doubled (see page 10).

- 3 tablespoons canola oil
- 2 scallions, white parts minced, green parts sliced thin
- 1 tablespoon curry powder
- 1 teaspoon grated fresh ginger
- 1 red bell pepper, stemmed, seeded, and cut into 2-inch-long matchsticks

- 1 carrot, peeled, halved lengthwise, and sliced thin on bias
- 12 ounces extra-large shrimp (21 to 25 per pound), peeled, deveined, and tails removed
- 4 ounces rice vermicelli
- 1½ tablespoons soy sauce

- 1 teaspoon lime juice, plus lime wedges for serving
- 2 ounces (1 cup) bean sprouts
- ½ cup fresh cilantro leaves and stems, chopped

1 Whisk oil, scallion whites, curry powder, and ginger together in large bowl. Microwave until fragrant, about 30 seconds.

2 Toss bell pepper and carrot with 1 teaspoon oil mixture in separate bowl. Arrange vegetables in even layer in air-fryer basket. Place basket into air fryer and set temperature to 400 degrees. Cook until vegetables are softened and lightly browned, 10 to 15 minutes, tossing halfway through cooking.

3 Halve shrimp lengthwise. Toss shrimp with 1 teaspoon oil mixture in now-empty bowl. Arrange shrimp in even layer on top of vegetables. Return basket to air fryer and cook until shrimp are opaque throughout, 6 to 10 minutes, flipping shrimp halfway through cooking.

4 Meanwhile, place noodles in large bowl or container and cover with boiling water. Let sit, stirring occasionally, until noodles are tender, about 5 minutes. Drain noodles well. Whisk soy sauce and lime juice into remaining oil mixture. Add noodles, vegetable-shrimp mixture, bean sprouts, cilantro, and scallion greens and toss gently to combine. Serve with lime wedges.

Per Serving Cal 540 | Total Fat 24g | Sat Fat 2g | Chol 160mg | Sodium 940mg
Total Carb 58g | Dietary Fiber 5g | Total Sugars 6g | Added Sugars 0g | Protein 24g

CHIPOTLE SHRIMP TACOS

Serves 2 | Total Time: 45 minutes

Why This Recipe Works Shrimp cook quickly, but with the air fryer we could set the timer and not worry about them overcooking and getting chewy. For these tacos, we paired them with fresh, crunchy cabbage; cilantro; and a light lime yogurt. Flavor also came from smoky canned chipotles, with which we coated the shrimp after cutting them in half lengthwise to coat more surface area. We quickly pickled thinly sliced onion in brine and used the pickling liquid to dress the shredded cabbage and cilantro. Large shrimp (26 to 30 per pound) will also work here; adjust the cooking time as needed. You can lightly char the tortillas, one at a time, over a gas burner or stack tortillas, wrap tightly in aluminum foil, and warm in the air fryer set to 350 degrees for 5 minutes, flipping halfway through cooking. Serve with queso fresco and diced avocado. This recipe can be easily doubled (see page 10).

½ cup distilled white vinegar

2 tablespoons packed light brown sugar, divided

½ teaspoon table salt, divided

½ small red onion, sliced thin

12 ounces extra-large shrimp (21 to 25 per pound), peeled, deveined, and tails removed

2 tablespoons minced canned chipotle chile in adobo sauce

1 tablespoon extra-virgin olive oil

½ teaspoon chili powder

¼ cup plain Greek yogurt

1 tablespoon lime juice, plus lime wedges for serving

1½ cups shredded napa cabbage

¼ cup chopped fresh cilantro, plus extra leaves for serving

6 (6-inch) corn tortillas, warmed

1 Microwave vinegar, 1½ tablespoons sugar, and ¼ teaspoon salt in medium bowl until steaming, 2 to 3 minutes; whisk to dissolve sugar and salt. Add onion to hot brine and press to submerge completely. Let sit for 45 minutes. Drain, reserving 2 tablespoons brine. (Drained onion and reserved brine can be refrigerated for up to 1 week.)

2 Lightly spray air-fryer basket with canola oil spray. Halve shrimp lengthwise. Combine chipotle, oil, chili powder, remaining 1½ teaspoons sugar, and remaining ¼ teaspoon salt in large bowl. Add shrimp and toss to coat. Arrange shrimp in even layer in prepared basket. Place basket into air fryer and set temperature to 400 degrees. Cook until shrimp are opaque throughout, 6 to 10 minutes, tossing halfway through cooking.

3 Whisk yogurt and lime juice together in small bowl. Toss cabbage with cilantro and reserved brine in separate bowl. Serve shrimp with warmed tortillas, cabbage, pickled onion, yogurt, lime wedges, and extra cilantro leaves.

Per Serving Cal 420 | Total Fat 14g | Sat Fat 3.5g | Chol 165mg | Sodium 670mg
Total Carb 47g | Dietary Fiber 5g | Total Sugars 10g | Added Sugars 7g | Protein 24g

VEGETABLE MAINS AND SIDES

MAINS

120 Stuffed Portobello Mushrooms with Kale, Corn, and Pickled Jalapeños

122 White Bean and Mushroom Gratin

125 Roasted Butternut Squash Salad with Za'atar and Halloumi

126 Ramen Noodle Bowl with Eggplant and Five-Spice Tofu

128 Make-Ahead Lentil and Mushroom Burgers
with Radicchio and Pear Salad

SIDES

131 Roasted Broccoli
with Parmesan, Lemon, and Black Pepper Topping
with Sesame and Lime Topping

132 Roasted Eggplant with Capers, Oregano, and Garlic

135 Roasted Fennel with Orange-Honey Dressing

136 Roasted Leeks with Almonds, Dried Cherries, and Balsamic Vinaigrette

139 Roasted Mushrooms with Shallot and Thyme

140 Roasted Sweet Potato Wedges

143 Roasted Potatoes with Parsley, Lemon, and Garlic

144 Crispy Baked Potato Fans

147 Roasted Delicata Squash
Spicy Maple Syrup
Goat Cheese and Chive Sauce

STUFFED PORTOBELLO MUSHROOMS WITH KALE, CORN, AND PICKLED JALAPEÑOS

Serves 2 | Total Time: 45 minutes

Why This Recipe Works For a healthy vegetable main that meat eaters and vegetarians alike would enjoy, we packed meaty portobellos with a combination of earthy kale, smoky fire-roasted corn, spicy jalapeños, and creamy yogurt. We started by using a spoon to gently scrape off the feathery dark gills from the underside of each portobello cap, which resulted in a pleasant, smooth texture. Next, we roasted the mushrooms until they were tender and then filled them with the vegetable goodness that complemented their savoriness. Finally, we topped them with crunchy panko bread crumbs and heated the dish through. These mushrooms are satisfying and flavorful, especially when served with the sauce that echoes the ingredients in the filling. If fire-roasted corn is unavailable, substitute traditional frozen corn; avoid canned corn here. For a spicier filling, use the greater amount of jalapeños.

- 7 tablespoons plain Greek yogurt, divided
- 2 teaspoons lime juice, plus lime wedges for serving
- 1 teaspoon chili powder, divided
- ¼ teaspoon honey
- ⅛ teaspoon plus ¼ teaspoon table salt, divided

- 4 portobello mushroom caps (4 to 5 inches in diameter), gills removed
- Olive oil spray
- ¼ cup panko bread crumbs
- 1 teaspoon plus 2 tablespoons extra-virgin olive oil, divided

- 2 cups frozen chopped kale or spinach, thawed and squeezed dry
- 1 cup frozen fire-roasted corn, thawed
- 2-4 tablespoons minced jarred jalapeños

1 Whisk ¼ cup yogurt, lime juice, ½ teaspoon chili powder, honey, and ⅛ teaspoon salt together in bowl. Season with salt and pepper to taste; set aside for serving.

2 Lightly spray mushrooms with oil spray and arrange gill side down in air-fryer basket. (Mushrooms will overlap and basket will seem quite full at first; mushrooms will shrink down substantially while cooking.) Place basket into air fryer and set temperature to 400 degrees. Cook until mushrooms are tender, 8 to 10 minutes.

3 Toss panko with 1 teaspoon oil in small bowl until evenly coated. Microwave, stirring frequently, until light golden brown, 1 to 3 minutes. Whisk remaining 3 tablespoons yogurt, remaining ½ teaspoon chili powder, remaining ¼ teaspoon salt, and remaining 2 tablespoons oil together in large bowl. Stir in kale, corn, and jalapeños.

4 Transfer mushrooms to cutting board, gill side up; pat dry with paper towels. Distribute filling evenly among mushrooms and sprinkle with panko, pressing gently to adhere. Arrange mushrooms in now-empty basket; place basket into air fryer; and cook until mushrooms are heated through, 5 to 7 minutes. Serve with sauce and lime wedges.

Per Serving Cal 400 | Total Fat 24g | Sat Fat 7g | Chol 10mg | Sodium 740mg
Total Carb 38g | Dietary Fiber 5g | Total Sugars 9g | Added Sugars 1g | Protein 13g

WHITE BEAN AND MUSHROOM GRATIN

Serves 2 | Total Time: 45 minutes

Why This Recipe Works A gratin is a dish of seasoned potatoes or other vegetables topped with bread crumbs or cheese and baked till the crust is crisp and golden. For our sumptuous gratin sized for two, we used protein-rich white beans, meaty cremini mushrooms, and zucchini flavored with tart tomato paste, soy sauce, and thyme. To make our vegetable gratin hearty, we opted to use bread cubes instead of bread crumbs. The larger chunks made the topping a blend of chewy and toasty. We used a pan to hold the ingredients so that the liquid could flavor the vegetables and create a sauce, which we thickened with a combination of flour and the starchy canned bean liquid. The sauce's flavor came from browning the mushrooms and shallot before assembling the gratin. We topped the gratin with lightly seasoned and oiled bread cubes and baked it at a low temperature. The lower portion of the bread merged with the vegetables, creating a pleasantly soft texture, while the upper portion became golden brown and crisp. You will need a 6-inch round nonstick or silicone cake pan for this recipe; before starting this recipe, confirm your air fryer allows enough space for the pan.

8 ounces cremini mushrooms, trimmed and sliced ½ inch thick

1 large shallot, sliced thin

2 tablespoons extra-virgin olive oil, divided, plus extra for drizzling

1 tablespoon tomato paste

1½ teaspoons all-purpose flour

1 (15-ounce) can cannellini or great northern beans, undrained

1 small zucchini, cut into ½-inch pieces

2 tablespoons water

1 teaspoon soy sauce

1 teaspoon minced fresh thyme or ¼ teaspoon dried

¼ teaspoon pepper

1 slice rustic whole-grain bread, cut into ½-inch pieces (1 cup)

1 tablespoon minced fresh parsley

1 Toss mushrooms, shallot, 1 tablespoon oil, tomato paste, and flour together in large bowl; transfer to air-fryer basket. Place basket into air fryer and set temperature to 400 degrees. Cook until mushrooms are tender and lightly browned, 8 to 10 minutes, tossing halfway through cooking.

2 Transfer vegetables to now-empty bowl. Add beans and their liquid, zucchini, water, soy sauce, thyme, and pepper and toss to combine. Transfer vegetable mixture to 6-inch round nonstick or silicone cake pan and spread into even layer. Toss bread with remaining 1 tablespoon oil in now-empty bowl; spread evenly over vegetable mixture.

3 Place pan in air-fryer basket and place basket into air fryer. Set temperature to 300 degrees and cook until sauce is bubbling around edges and topping is golden brown, 15 to 20 minutes. Remove pan from basket and let cool slightly. Sprinkle with parsley and drizzle with extra oil. Serve.

Per Serving Cal 450 | Total Fat 16g | Sat Fat 2.5g | Chol 0mg | Sodium 900mg
Total Carb 59g | Dietary Fiber 12g | Total Sugars 11g | Added Sugars 0g | Protein 22g

ROASTED BUTTERNUT SQUASH SALAD WITH ZA'ATAR AND HALLOUMI

Serves 2 | Total Time: 45 minutes

Why This Recipe Works For a main-dish vegetarian salad, we air-fried butternut squash, making it golden brown and tender in less than half the time it would take in a conventional oven. Roasting enhanced the squash's sweetness; za'atar, a Middle Eastern blend that often contains dried thyme, sumac, and sesame seeds, added woodsy notes. We paired the squash with halloumi, a firm, salty Cypriot cheese that's traditionally grilled but crisps up beautifully in the air fryer. If you can't find halloumi, you can finish the dish with crumbled feta (but skip cooking the cheese in step 2). A lemon-honey dressing gave the salad brightness, and pepitas added protein, fiber, and crunch. This recipe can be easily doubled (see page 10).

- 1 small shallot, minced
- 1 teaspoon grated lemon zest plus 2 tablespoons juice
- 2 pounds butternut squash, peeled, seeded, and cut into 1-inch pieces (6 cups)

- 4 teaspoons extra-virgin olive oil, divided
- 2 teaspoons za'atar
- ½ teaspoon table salt
- Olive oil spray
- 2 ounces halloumi cheese, cut into ½-inch pieces and patted dry

- 2 teaspoons honey
- ¼ teaspoon pepper
- 2 ounces (2 cups) baby arugula
- ¼ cup roasted, unsalted pepitas
- 2 tablespoons chopped fresh dill

1 Combine shallot and lemon juice in small bowl; set aside. Toss squash with 1 teaspoon oil, za'atar, and salt in large bowl. Arrange squash in even layer in air-fryer basket. Place basket into air fryer; set temperature to 400 degrees; and cook until squash is just tender and browned in spots, 16 to 22 minutes, tossing twice during cooking.

2 Return squash to large bowl; set aside. Lightly spray base of now-empty basket with oil spray, scatter halloumi in basket, and lightly spray halloumi with oil spray. Return basket to fryer and cook until halloumi is browned around edges, 4 to 6 minutes.

3 Whisk honey, pepper, lemon zest, and remaining 1 tablespoon oil into shallot mixture. Add to squash and toss to coat. Add arugula, pepitas, and dill and toss to combine. Season with salt and pepper to taste. Transfer to serving platter, top with halloumi, and serve.

Per Serving Cal 400 | Total Fat 25g | Sat Fat 8g | Chol 20mg | Sodium 910mg
Total Carb 57g | Dietary Fiber 10g | Total Sugars 16g | Added Sugars 5g | Protein 15g

RAMEN NOODLE BOWL WITH EGGPLANT AND FIVE-SPICE TOFU

Serves 2 | Total Time: 45 minutes

Why This Recipe Works Inspired by ramen, we wanted to develop a satisfying vegetarian noodle bowl mounded high with eggplant and crispy tofu. This was not a dish that screamed air fryer, but we used it to cook the eggplant and fry the tofu, leaving our hands free to whisk together a dressing and soak dried ramen noodles in boiling water. Eggplant batons coated with soy sauce, mirin, and toasted sesame oil became appetizingly silky in the air fryer. Draining our tofu on paper towels removed excess moisture so that the exterior of the cubes could crisp up, and tossing them with cornmeal (instead of cornstarch) gave them added crunch. Five-spice powder and soy sauce brought flavor to the dish, as did the rice vinegar, mirin, and ginger dressing. Despite the package instructions, the noodles need only a quick soak in boiling water to become tender. The large bowl in step 2 is reused several times in this recipe; there is no need to clean it. This recipe can be easily doubled (see page 10).

- 7 ounces firm or extra-firm tofu, cut into 1-inch pieces
- 1 eggplant (1 pound)
- 2 tablespoons mirin, divided
- 1 tablespoon soy sauce, divided
- 1 tablespoon toasted sesame oil, divided
- 2 teaspoons cornmeal
- ¾ teaspoon five-spice powder
- ¼ teaspoon table salt
- 4 teaspoons unseasoned rice vinegar
- 2 scallions, white parts minced, green parts sliced thin on bias
- 1 teaspoon grated fresh ginger
- 2 (3-ounce) packages ramen noodles, seasoning packets discarded
- 2 radishes, sliced thin

1 Spread tofu on paper towel–lined plate, let drain for 20 minutes, then press dry gently with paper towels.

2 Meanwhile, slice eggplant lengthwise into ¾-inch-thick planks. Halve each plank crosswise, then cut lengthwise into ¾-inch-wide strips. Whisk 1 tablespoon mirin, 1 teaspoon soy sauce, and 1 teaspoon oil together in large bowl. Add eggplant and toss to coat; transfer to air-fryer basket. Place basket into air fryer and set temperature to 400 degrees. Cook until eggplant is softened and lightly browned, 10 to 15 minutes, tossing halfway through cooking.

3 Transfer eggplant to plate; set aside. Toss tofu with cornmeal, five-spice powder, salt, and 1 teaspoon oil in now-empty bowl until evenly coated. Arrange tofu in even layer in now-empty basket. Return basket to air fryer and cook until tofu is crisp and lightly browned, 10 to 15 minutes, tossing halfway through cooking.

4 Meanwhile, whisk vinegar, 1 tablespoon water, scallion whites, ginger, remaining 1 tablespoon mirin, remaining 2 teaspoons soy sauce, and remaining 1 teaspoon oil together in small bowl. Place ramen in again-empty large bowl; cover with boiling water; and let sit until softened, about 5 minutes, stirring occasionally to separate noodles.

5 Drain noodles thoroughly and return to large bowl. Add dressing and toss to coat. Divide noodles between 2 serving bowls and top with any remaining dressing in bowl, eggplant, tofu, and radishes. Sprinkle with scallion greens and serve.

Per Serving Cal 540 | Total Fat 15g | Sat Fat 2g | Chol 0mg | Sodium 760mg
Total Carb 86g | Dietary Fiber 6g | Total Sugars 11g | Added Sugars 0g | Protein 23g

MAKE-AHEAD LENTIL AND MUSHROOM BURGERS

Makes 6 patties | Total Time: 45 minutes

Why This Recipe Works The complex flavor and satisfying texture of this vegetarian burger is well worth the prep. Using the air fryer to cook the patties meant that they were ready from fresh or frozen in just 10 minutes. An earthy mix of canned lentils, bulgur, and panko paired with shallot and celery gave our burgers a flavorful, hearty meatless base. Cremini mushrooms and a surprising addition—chopped cashews—created rich meatiness. Chopping everything in the food processor made for a cohesive and even-textured mix, and olive oil provided fat to bind the patties. Microwaving the mixture helped soften the bulgur and allowed the flavors to meld. Look for medium-grind bulgur (labeled "#2"), which is roughly the size of mustard seeds. Avoid coarsely ground bulgur; it will not cook through in time. The number of patties you can cook at one time will depend on the size of your air fryer. Serve with your favorite toppings and roasted sweet potato wedges (page 140), if desired.

- 8 ounces cremini or white mushrooms, trimmed and quartered
- ½ cup raw cashews
- 1 celery rib, cut into 1-inch pieces
- 1 shallot, quartered
- ½ cup medium-grind bulgur
- ¼ cup water
- 3 tablespoons extra-virgin olive oil
- ½ teaspoon table salt
- 1 (15-ounce) can brown lentils, rinsed
- ½ cup panko bread crumbs
- 1–6 slices deli cheese (optional)
- 1–6 hamburger buns, toasted if desired

1 Pulse mushrooms, cashews, celery, and shallot in food processor until finely chopped, about 10 pulses, scraping down sides of bowl as needed. Transfer vegetables to large bowl and stir in bulgur, water, oil, and salt. Microwave, stirring occasionally, until bulgur is softened and most of liquid has been absorbed, about 6 minutes. Let cool slightly.

2 Lightly spray base of air-fryer basket with canola oil spray. Vigorously stir lentils and panko into vegetable-bulgur mixture until well combined and mixture forms cohesive mass. Using your lightly moistened hands, divide mixture into 6 equal portions (about ½ cup each), then tightly pack each portion into ½-inch-thick patty.

3 Space up to 4 patties at least ½ inch apart in prepared basket. Place basket into air fryer and set temperature to 400 degrees. Cook until patties are golden brown and crisp, 10 to 15 minutes. Turn off air fryer. Top each burger with 1 slice cheese, if using; let sit in warm air fryer until melted, about 1 minute. If desired, arrange bun tops and bottoms cut side up in now-empty basket. Return basket to air fryer, set temperature to 400, and cook until buns are lightly toasted, 4 to 6 minutes. Serve burgers on buns.

4 Evenly space any remaining patties on parchment paper–lined rimmed baking sheet and freeze until firm, about 1 hour. Stack patties between pieces of parchment, wrap in plastic wrap, and place in zipper-lock freezer bag. Patties can be frozen for up to 1 month. Cook frozen patties as directed; do not thaw.

MAKE-AHEAD LENTIL AND MUSHROOM BURGERS WITH RADICCHIO AND PEAR SALAD

The radicchio and pear salad makes enough for two burgers; it can be easily doubled or tripled.

Whisk 2 teaspoons oil, 1 teaspoon Dijon mustard, 1 teaspoon honey, ⅛ teaspoon table salt, and ⅛ teaspoon pepper in separate large bowl. Add 1 cup shredded radicchio and ½ ripe but firm pear, cored and cut into 2-inch-long matchsticks, and toss until evenly coated. Omit deli cheese. Spread 2 tablespoons softened goat cheese on each bun top. Serve burgers on buns, topped with radicchio and pear salad.

Per Serving Cal 350 | Total Fat 14g | Sat Fat 2g | Chol 0mg | Sodium 490mg
Total Carb 47g | Dietary Fiber 6g | Total Sugars 6g | Added Sugars 0g | Protein 12g

ROASTED BROCCOLI

Serves 2 | Total Time: 20 minutes

Why This Recipe Works The nutty crispness of roasted broccoli is irresistible. For a healthy side you can't stop eating, we air-fried the vegetable quickly. We cut broccoli florets into 2-inch pieces. To cook, flavor, and crisp up vegetables such as broccoli in the air fryer, we learned that tossing them with water and oil does the trick. Oil and water together might seem counterintuitive, but here's what happens: The water steams the vegetable initially to soften it, and when the water evaporates, the oil provides optimal heat transfer and browning. We drizzled the cooked broccoli with a little more oil before serving. To preserve the crispness in our variations, we sprinkled the roasted broccoli with toppings that added flavor and texture rather than a liquid finish that would make them soggy. This recipe can be easily doubled (see page 10).

1 tablespoon water

1 tablespoon extra-virgin olive oil, plus extra for drizzling

¼ teaspoon table salt

1 pound broccoli florets, cut into 2-inch pieces

Lemon wedges

Whisk water, oil, and salt in large bowl until salt has dissolved. Add broccoli and toss to coat; transfer to air-fryer basket and spread into even layer. Place basket into air fryer and set temperature to 350 degrees. Cook until broccoli is well browned and tender, 8 to 12 minutes, tossing halfway through cooking. Transfer broccoli to serving platter and drizzle with extra oil. Serve with lemon wedges.

ROASTED BROCCOLI WITH PARMESAN, LEMON, AND BLACK PEPPER TOPPING

Omit lemon wedges. Using your fingers, mix ½ teaspoon pepper and ½ teaspoon grated lemon zest in small bowl until evenly combined. Add ½ cup grated Parmesan and toss with your fingers or fork until pepper and lemon zest are evenly distributed. Transfer roasted broccoli to serving platter and sprinkle with topping before serving.

ROASTED BROCCOLI WITH SESAME AND LIME TOPPING

Omit lemon wedges. Substitute toasted sesame oil for extra-virgin olive oil. Using your fingers, mix 2 tablespoons toasted sesame seeds, ½ teaspoon grated lime zest, and pinch table salt in small bowl until evenly combined. Transfer roasted broccoli to serving platter and sprinkle with topping before serving.

Per Serving Cal 130 | Total Fat 8g | Sat Fat 1g | Chol 0mg | Sodium 350mg
Total Carb 11g | Dietary Fiber 5g | Total Sugars 3g | Added Sugars 0g | Protein 7g

ROASTED EGGPLANT WITH CAPERS, OREGANO, AND GARLIC

Serves 2 | Total Time: 30 minutes

Why This Recipe Works Marinated eggplant is a classic Middle Eastern dish that's great as an appetizer or a side with summery main dishes. To keep the eggplant in the spotlight and reduce the amount of oil used for frying and marinating it, we roasted it instead and replaced the marinade with a brightly flavored dressing. We chose baby eggplants, which are smaller than the standard supermarket size, are more readily available in the summer months, and cook quickly. Roasting helped us achieve flavorful browning on the eggplant. To keep the dressing delicate, a Greek-inspired combination of just a tablespoon of extra-virgin olive oil, fragrant lemon zest and juice, capers, oregano, and garlic worked perfectly. If baby eggplant is unavailable, one 1-pound eggplant can be substituted; halve it lengthwise before slicing it crosswise. This recipe can be easily doubled (see page 10).

2 baby eggplants (8 to 10 ounces each), sliced into 1-inch-thick rounds

Olive oil spray

¼ teaspoon table salt

⅛ teaspoon pepper

1 tablespoon extra-virgin olive oil

1 teaspoon capers, rinsed and minced

1 teaspoon minced fresh oregano

1 small garlic clove, minced

½ teaspoon grated lemon zest plus 2 teaspoons juice

1 Lightly spray both sides of eggplant with oil spray and sprinkle with salt and pepper. Arrange eggplant in even layer in air-fryer basket (pieces may overlap). Place basket into air fryer and set temperature to 350 degrees. Cook until eggplant is deep golden brown, 16 to 20 minutes, flipping eggplant halfway through cooking.

2 Whisk oil, capers, oregano, garlic, and lemon zest and juice together in large bowl. Add eggplant and toss gently to combine. Serve warm or at room temperature. (Eggplant can be refrigerated for up to 3 days. Let come to room temperature before serving.)

Per Serving Cal 120 | Total Fat 7g | Sat Fat 1g | Chol 0mg | Sodium 330mg
Total Carb 15g | Dietary Fiber 6g | Total Sugars 7g | Added Sugars 0g | Protein 2g

ROASTED FENNEL WITH ORANGE-HONEY DRESSING

Serves 2 | Total Time: 30 minutes

Why This Recipe Works The short roasting time needed for fennel in the air fryer helps retain its nutrients and anise flavor. We began by cutting the bulb into wedges, which had two benefits: It provided good surface area for browning, and the attached core kept the pieces intact. Tossing the wedges with salted water and oil allowed them to steam and turn creamy during the first part of cooking; it also allowed seasoning to get between their layers. Once the water evaporated, the oil helped turn the wedges golden and deliciously caramelized. The orange and honey in the dressing enhanced the sweetness of the roasted fennel. Look for a fennel bulb that measures 3½ to 4 inches in diameter and weighs around 1 pound with the stalks; trim the base very lightly so that the bulb remains intact. If your fennel does not have fronds, omit them. This recipe can be easily doubled (see page 10).

1 fennel bulb, base lightly trimmed, 2 tablespoons fronds chopped coarse, stalks discarded

2 tablespoons extra-virgin olive oil, divided

1 tablespoon water

¼ teaspoon table salt

¼ teaspoon pepper

2 teaspoons honey

1½ teaspoons white wine vinegar

⅛ teaspoon grated orange zest plus 1 tablespoon juice

1 Cut fennel bulb lengthwise through core into 8 wedges (do not remove core). Whisk 1 tablespoon oil, water, salt, and pepper in large bowl until salt has dissolved. Add fennel wedges and toss gently to coat.

2 Arrange fennel wedges cut side down in air-fryer basket (wedges may overlap). Place basket into air fryer and set temperature to 350 degrees. Cook until fennel is tender and well browned, 12 to 20 minutes, flipping wedges halfway through cooking.

3 Whisk fennel fronds, honey, vinegar, orange zest and juice, and remaining 1 tablespoon oil together in bowl. Season with salt and pepper to taste. Transfer fennel to serving platter and drizzle with dressing. Serve.

Per Serving Cal 190 | Total Fat 14g | Sat Fat 2g | Chol 0mg | Sodium 350mg
Total Carb 15g | Dietary Fiber 4g | Total Sugars 11g | Added Sugars 5g | Protein 2g

ROASTED LEEKS WITH ALMONDS, DRIED CHERRIES, AND BALSAMIC VINAIGRETTE

Serves 2 | Total Time: 30 minutes

Why This Recipe Works Leeks make an elegant side dish. During testing, we found that if the heat was too high, the leeks' outer layers scorched before the interiors softened. If too low, the leeks dried out and toughened up. Roasting at 375 degrees and adding some boiling water to the air-fryer base helped retain the vegetable's moisture, keeping it tender. Washing the leeks just before cooking trapped some water between the layers, helping them steam from the inside. A balsamic vinaigrette, almonds, and dried cherries really elevated the dish. Look for leeks that are 1 to 1¼ inches in diameter at the base; they are more tender. If using larger leeks, peel away the outer layers to achieve the correct size. For an accurate measurement of boiling water, bring a kettle of water to a boil and then measure out the desired amount. If using an air-fryer lid for a multicooker, pour the water directly into the pot in step 1; if using an air-fryer oven, pour the water onto the drip tray. For more information on toasting nuts, see page 12. This recipe can be easily doubled (see page 10); do not increase the water in step 1.

2 leeks, white and light green parts only, halved lengthwise

4 teaspoons extra-virgin olive oil, divided

¼ teaspoon table salt, divided

½ cup boiling water

1½ teaspoons balsamic vinegar

⅛ teaspoon pepper

1 tablespoon chopped toasted whole almonds, hazelnuts, pecans, or walnuts

1 tablespoon dried cherries, raisins, or dried apricots, chopped

1 Cut each leek half in half crosswise and wash thoroughly, taking care to keep layers intact. Toss pieces gently with 1 teaspoon oil in bowl and sprinkle with ⅛ teaspoon salt. Pour boiling water into bottom of air-fryer drawer, then arrange leeks cut side down in basket (leeks may overlap slightly). Set temperature to 375 degrees and cook until leeks are very tender and well browned, 14 to 18 minutes, flipping leeks halfway through cooking.

2 Transfer leeks to serving platter and season with salt and pepper to taste. Whisk vinegar, pepper, remaining 1 tablespoon oil, and remaining ⅛ teaspoon salt together in small bowl. Drizzle vinaigrette over leeks and sprinkle with almonds and dried cherries. Serve warm or at room temperature.

Per Serving Cal 170 | Total Fat 11g | Sat Fat 1.5g | Chol 0mg | Sodium 310mg
Total Carb 18g | Dietary Fiber 2g | Total Sugars 8g | Added Sugars 0g | Protein 2g

ROASTED MUSHROOMS WITH SHALLOT AND THYME

Serves 2 | Total Time: 25 minutes

Why This Recipe Works We started with the classic combination of woodsy mushrooms, aromatic shallot, and earthy thyme. Air-frying allowed us to use less oil and prevented the mushrooms from losing too much liquid, as they might in a skillet. These tender roasted mushrooms pair beautifully with beef, fish, and tofu; can be served with other sides such as potatoes; and make a great topping for salads or bruschetta. To prevent the shallot from burning, we gave the mushrooms a head start, roasting them until they were softened and then adding the shallot for the final few minutes, until the mushrooms were well browned (but still juicy) and the shallot was softened and lightly browned. Meanwhile, we made an aromatic dressing to toss the cooked mushroom mixture in. Use a single variety of mushroom or a combination. Stem and halve portobello mushrooms and cut into ½-inch pieces. Trim white or cremini mushrooms; quarter them if they're large or medium or halve them if they're small. Tear trimmed oyster mushrooms into 1- to 1½-inch pieces. Stem shiitake mushrooms; quarter large caps and halve small caps. Cut trimmed maitake (hen of the woods) mushrooms into 1- to 1½-inch pieces. This recipe can be easily doubled (see page 10).

1 pound mushrooms

2 tablespoons extra-virgin olive oil, divided

¼ teaspoon table salt, divided

⅛ teaspoon pepper

1 shallot, sliced thin

2 teaspoons lemon juice

2 teaspoons minced fresh thyme, rosemary, oregano, marjoram, or sage

1 Toss mushrooms with 1 tablespoon oil, ⅛ teaspoon salt, and pepper in large bowl; arrange in even layer in air-fryer basket. Place basket into air fryer and set temperature to 400 degrees. Cook until mushrooms are softened, 8 to 12 minutes, tossing halfway through cooking.

2 Stir shallot into mushrooms. Return basket to air fryer and cook until mushrooms are well browned, 2 to 4 minutes.

3 Whisk lemon juice, thyme, remaining 1 tablespoon oil, and remaining ⅛ teaspoon salt together in now-empty bowl. Add mushroom mixture and toss to coat. Season with salt and pepper to taste. Serve.

Per Serving Cal 190 | Total Fat 14g | Sat Fat 2g | Chol 0mg | Sodium 310mg
Total Carb 10g | Dietary Fiber 1g | Total Sugars 7g | Added Sugars 0g | Protein 4g

ROASTED SWEET POTATO WEDGES

Serves 2 | Total Time: 30 minutes

Why This Recipe Works These sweet potato wedges are as indulgent to eat as restaurant sweet potato fries but healthy because you made them at home with only a little oil and no deep frying. Sweet potatoes release a sweet, syrupy liquid as they cook, and this turned the wedges mushy. The key was to leave the sweet potatoes unpeeled and cut them into wide wedges so that they would hold their shape while roasting. This worked well because the skins are delicious, and they're also rich in vitamins, minerals, and fiber. Cut thinner, the wedges burned before their interiors had the chance to cook through. Since sweet potatoes have plenty of flavor on their own, we limited the seasoning to salt, pepper, and a little olive oil to encourage browning. After about 20 minutes in the air fryer, the sweet potatoes were perfectly creamy and sweet on the inside, with plenty of crunch on the outside. We prefer to use small potatoes, about 8 ounces each, because this ensures that the wedges fit more uniformly in the air-fryer basket; they should be of similar size so that they cook at the same rate. Be sure to scrub and dry the whole potatoes thoroughly before cutting them into wedges and tossing them with the oil and spices.

1 pound small sweet potatoes (8 ounces each), unpeeled, cut lengthwise into 1½-inch wedges

1 tablespoon extra-virgin olive oil

¼ teaspoon table salt

¼ teaspoon pepper

Toss all ingredients together in bowl and arrange in even layer in air-fryer basket. Place basket into air fryer and set temperature to 350 degrees. Cook until lightly browned and tender, 20 to 25 minutes, tossing halfway through cooking. Serve.

Per Serving Cal 200 | Total Fat 7g | Sat Fat 1g | Chol 0mg | Sodium 380mg
Total Carb 33g | Dietary Fiber 5g | Total Sugars 7g | Added Sugars 0g | Protein 3g

ROASTED POTATOES WITH PARSLEY, LEMON, AND GARLIC

Serves 2 | Total Time: 35 minutes

Why This Recipe Works To roast potatoes in the high heat of the air fryer and achieve creamy tenderness, we chose small red or Yukon Gold potatoes, which are better able to retain moisture than classic baking, or high-starch, potatoes. Keeping the skin on provided more fiber. We tossed the cut potatoes with oil and arranged them in the air-fryer basket, where they fit snugly in a single layer. Shaking the basket halfway through roasting ensured that the browning was even. Tossing the potatoes with parsley, lemon zest, and garlic after they were cooked prevented the parsley from burning in the air fryer and allowed us to disperse the ingredients more evenly over the potatoes. Use small potatoes measuring 1 to 2 inches in diameter.

- 1 pound small red or Yukon Gold potatoes, unpeeled, halved
- 1 tablespoon extra-virgin olive oil
- ¼ teaspoon table salt
- ¼ teaspoon pepper
- 1 tablespoon chopped fresh parsley
- 1 teaspoon grated lemon zest
- 1 small garlic clove, minced

1 Toss potatoes with oil, salt, and pepper in bowl and arrange in even layer in air-fryer basket. Place basket into air fryer and set temperature to 400 degrees. Cook until potatoes are tender, well browned, and crisp, 25 to 30 minutes, tossing halfway through cooking.

2 Transfer potatoes to now-empty bowl and toss with parsley, lemon zest, and garlic until evenly coated. Season with salt and pepper to taste. Serve.

Per Serving Cal 230 | Total Fat 7g | Sat Fat 1g | Chol 0mg | Sodium 330mg
Total Carb 37g | Dietary Fiber 4g | Total Sugars 3g | Added Sugars 0g | Protein 4g

CRISPY BAKED POTATO FANS

Serves 2 | Total Time: 45 minutes

Why This Recipe Works Essentially baked potatoes but par-sliced into thin, even segments that create a fanlike shape, our air-fried potato fans become extra-crispy on the outside while their interiors remain fluffy and moist. This impressive potato dish—believed to have originated in Sweden at the Hasselbacken restaurant—is surprisingly easy to prepare. For a healthy take on a classic often loaded with butter, sour cream, cheese, or other rich toppings, we turned to heart-healthy olive oil to help crisp the segments and added flavor with aromatic smoked paprika and garlic powder instead. We found that using the right kind of potato was key. The russet, or Idaho, potato was the best choice because of its starchy flesh and creamy texture. Taking the time to rinse the potatoes of surface starch after they were sliced prevented them from sticking together, and trimming off the ends of each potato gave the slices room to fan out. To prevent overcooking or burning our spuds in the heat of the air fryer, we precooked them briefly in the microwave. To ensure that the potatoes fan out evenly, look for uniformly shaped potatoes. Chopsticks or thick skewers provide a foolproof guide for slicing the potato petals without cutting all the way through the potato in step 1.

2 russet potatoes, unpeeled

2 tablespoons extra-virgin olive oil

¼ teaspoon smoked paprika

¼ teaspoon garlic powder

¼ teaspoon table salt, divided

⅛ teaspoon pepper

2 tablespoons minced scallions, fresh chives, fresh dill, and/or fresh parsley

Lemon wedges

1 Cut ¼ inch from bottoms and ends of potatoes. Place 1 chopstick or thick skewer lengthwise on each side of 1 potato, then slice potato crosswise at ¼-inch intervals, stopping ¼ inch from bottom of potato. Repeat with second potato. Rinse potatoes gently under running water, let drain, and transfer to plate. Microwave until slightly tender when squeezed gently, 6 to 12 minutes, flipping potatoes halfway through cooking.

2 Combine oil, paprika, garlic powder, salt, and pepper in bowl. Brush potatoes with portion of oil mixture, then drizzle remaining oil in between slices. Arrange potatoes cut side up in air-fryer basket, spaced evenly apart. Place basket into air fryer and set temperature to 400 degrees. Cook until potato skins are crisp and golden brown and potato interiors register 205 degrees, 25 to 30 minutes. Sprinkle potatoes with scallions and serve with lemon wedges.

Per Serving Cal 300 | Total Fat 14g | Sat Fat 2g | Chol 0mg | Sodium 300mg
Total Carb 40g | Dietary Fiber 3g | Total Sugars 2g | Added Sugars 0g | Protein 5g

ROASTED DELICATA SQUASH

Serves 2 | Total Time: 30 minutes

Why This Recipe Works To have another squash side dish in your back pocket, consider delicata. The air fryer enhanced its natural sweetness and also added toastiness. The air fryer sped up the cooking process, too, and tossing the unpeeled squash with a little oil aided in browning. Two sauces—a spicy maple syrup and a goat cheese and chive sauce—bring heat or add richness to the roasted squash. Delicata have thin, edible skin that needn't be removed; simply use a vegetable peeler to pare away any tough brown blemishes. You can substitute acorn squash for the delicata; quarter it lengthwise before slicing it.

- 1 delicata squash (12 to 16 ounces), ends trimmed, halved lengthwise, seeded, and sliced crosswise ½ inch thick
- 1 tablespoon extra-virgin olive oil
- ¼ teaspoon table salt
- 1 tablespoon minced fresh parsley

Toss squash with oil and salt in bowl; arrange in even layer in air-fryer basket. Place basket into air fryer and set temperature to 350 degrees. Cook until squash is tender and golden brown, 18 to 20 minutes, tossing halfway through cooking. Transfer squash to serving platter, sprinkle with parsley, and serve.

SPICY MAPLE SYRUP

We prefer vinegary Frank's RedHot Original Cayenne Pepper Sauce here. Do not substitute a thick hot sauce, such as sriracha; it will make the syrup too thick to drizzle.

Reduce salt to ⅛ teaspoon. Stir 2 tablespoons maple syrup and 1 tablespoon hot sauce together in medium bowl. Microwave until mixture comes to boil, about 30 seconds. Continue to microwave in 20-second intervals until mixture is reduced to 2 tablespoons, about 1 minute. Let cool for 10 minutes. Drizzle syrup over squash before serving.

GOAT CHEESE AND CHIVE SAUCE

Whisk ¼ cup crumbled goat cheese, 2 tablespoons milk, 2 teaspoons minced fresh chives, ¼ teaspoon grated lemon zest, and ½ teaspoon lemon juice in bowl until smooth. Add up to 1 tablespoon more milk, 1 teaspoon at a time, as needed to create sauce that is thick but pourable. Season with salt and pepper to taste. Let sit for 10 minutes. Drizzle sauce over squash before serving.

Per Serving Cal 120 | Total Fat 7g | Sat Fat 1g | Chol 0mg | Sodium 300mg
Total Carb 14g | Dietary Fiber 2g | Total Sugars 3g | Added Sugars 0g | Protein 1g

SMALL BITES

150 Lemon-Pepper Chicken Wings
Parmesan-Garlic Chicken Wings
Cilantro-Lime Chicken Wings

153 Red Curry Chicken Kebabs with
Peanut Dipping Sauce

154 Beef-and-Bulgur Meatballs with
Tahini-Yogurt Dipping Sauce

156 Make-Ahead Crispy Egg Rolls

158 Make-Ahead Phyllo Hand Pies with
Fennel, Olive, and Goat Cheese Filling
with Apple, Walnut, and Blue Cheese Filling

161 Ricotta Tartlets with Tomato-Basil
Topping
with Celery-Olive Topping

162 Asparagus Fries with Yogurt Sauce

165 Shoestring Fries
with Rosemary and Lemon Zest
with Coriander and Dill

166 Whole-Wheat Pita Chips
with Salt and Pepper
Buttermilk-Ranch Whole-Wheat Pita Chips
Ras el Hanout Whole-Wheat Pita Chips

169 Romesco

170 Crispy Barbecue Chickpeas
Crispy Coriander-Cumin Chickpeas
Crispy Smoked Paprika Chickpeas

173 Date-Almond Snack Bars

174 Almond, Cherry, and Chocolate
Trail Mix

LEMON-PEPPER CHICKEN WINGS

Serves 2 | **Total Time: 30 minutes**

Why This Recipe Works Once you make chicken wings in your air fryer, you may never go back to conventional frying or oven roasting again. With their delicate skin and paper-thin layer of fat, chicken wings are a perfect candidate for air frying. In the intense, evenly circulating heat, the fat renders as the skin crisps, then conveniently accumulates at the bottom of the air fryer without smoking up your kitchen. Rather than toss our wings in gloppy, sugar- or fat-heavy sauces, we tossed them with our choice of superflavorful combinations: simple lemon and pepper with herbs, slightly more complex Parmesan and garlic (to round out the lemon, pepper, and herbs), and feisty cilantro and lime with jalapeño. These added a lot of zing to the wings without compromising their perfectly crisped exteriors. If you buy chicken wings that are already split, with the tips removed, you will need only 1 pound. This recipe can be easily doubled (see page 10).

1¼ pounds chicken wings, halved at joints, wingtips discarded

⅛ teaspoon table salt

¼ teaspoon pepper

1 tablespoon grated lemon zest, plus lemon wedges for serving

1 tablespoon minced fresh parsley, dill, and/ or tarragon

1 Pat wings dry with paper towels and sprinkle with salt and pepper. Arrange wings in even layer in air-fryer basket. Place basket into air fryer and set temperature to 400 degrees. Cook until wings are golden brown and crisp, 18 to 24 minutes, flipping wings halfway through cooking.

2 Combine lemon zest and parsley in large bowl. Add wings and toss until evenly coated. Serve with lemon wedges.

PARMESAN-GARLIC CHICKEN WINGS
Add 1 tablespoon grated Parmesan cheese and 1 minced garlic clove to lemon zest–parsley mixture.

CILANTRO-LIME CHICKEN WINGS
Substitute lime zest and wedges for lemon and cilantro for parsley. Add 1 tablespoon minced jalapeño chile to lime zest–cilantro mixture.

Per Serving Cal 170 | Total Fat 11g | Sat Fat 3.5g | Chol 95mg | Sodium 1400mg
Total Carb 0g | Dietary Fiber 0g | Total Sugars 0g | Added Sugars 0g | Protein 16g

RED CURRY CHICKEN KEBABS WITH PEANUT DIPPING SAUCE

Serves 2 | Total Time: 30 minutes

Why This Recipe Works For an appetizer that could double as a light meal, "air-grilled" chicken kebabs are just the ticket. We took a cue from the herbal, savory flavors of Southeast Asian satay dishes (which vary widely in sweetness, aroma, spiciness, and richness) and used store-bought red curry paste as a starting point. We combined the paste with sugar, fish sauce, and lime zest and juice to achieve a balance of salty, sweet, sour, bitter, and umami. We used 2 tablespoons of the mixture to coat thin slices of chicken breast that were easy to thread onto skewers. The remaining mixture served as the base of a creamy peanut dipping sauce. We arranged the kebabs in the air fryer in two layers like Lincoln Logs (see page 5) to facilitate even cooking. After just 6 to 8 minutes (the time it took to make the sauce), the chicken was lightly browned and tender. This recipe can be easily doubled (see page 10).

- 2 tablespoons Thai red curry paste
- 1 tablespoon packed brown sugar
- 2 teaspoons fish sauce
- 1 teaspoon grated lime zest plus 1 tablespoon juice, plus lime wedges for serving
- 12 ounces boneless, skinless chicken breasts
- 2 teaspoons canola oil
- 12 (6-inch) wooden skewers
- 3 tablespoons smooth peanut butter
- 2 tablespoons chopped fresh basil or cilantro

1 Whisk curry paste, sugar, fish sauce, and lime zest and juice together in large bowl. Transfer 2 tablespoons curry paste mixture to medium bowl; set aside.

2 Slice each chicken breast lengthwise ¼ inch thick (you should have at least 12 slices) and pat dry with paper towels. Whisk oil into remaining curry paste mixture in large bowl. Add chicken and toss to coat. Weave chicken slices evenly onto each skewer, leaving 1 inch at bottom of skewer exposed. (Kebabs and reserved curry paste mixture can be refrigerated separately for up to 24 hours.)

3 Arrange half of kebabs in air-fryer basket, parallel to each other and spaced evenly apart. Arrange remaining skewers on top, perpendicular to bottom layer. Place basket into air fryer and set temperature to 400 degrees. Cook until chicken is spotty browned, 6 to 8 minutes.

4 Whisk peanut butter into reserved curry paste mixture until smooth and sauce has consistency of heavy cream. Adjust consistency with hot water as needed. Transfer kebabs to serving platter and sprinkle with basil. Serve with sauce and lime wedges.

Per Serving Cal 230 | Total Fat 11g | Sat Fat 2g | Chol 60mg | Sodium 460mg
Total Carb 10g | Dietary Fiber 1g | Total Sugars 5g | Added Sugars 3g | Protein 23g

BEEF-AND-BULGUR MEATBALLS WITH TAHINI-YOGURT DIPPING SAUCE

Serves 2 | Total Time: 35 minutes

Why This Recipe Works These meatballs are so flavorful that they're bound to make their way onto your cocktail party menu time and time again. We used bulgur instead of bread crumbs for the panade. Bulgur, a whole grain packed with vitamins, minerals, and fiber, and used to make tabbouleh, inspired our Mediterranean flavor profile. We also incorporated yogurt, first combining it with herbs, garlic, and lots of lemon, reserving some for a sauce, and then using the rest in our 90 percent lean ground beef alongside warm spices. While the formed meatballs took a quick trip to the air fryer (which develops beautiful browning), we added some tahini and a little water to the reserved yogurt mixture, giving the dipping sauce an added nuttiness. Look for medium-grind bulgur (labeled "#2"), which is roughly the size of mustard seeds. Avoid coarsely ground bulgur; it will not cook through in time. For an accurate measurement of boiling water, bring a half kettle of water to a boil and then measure out the desired amount. This recipe can be easily doubled (see page 10).

¼ cup medium-grind bulgur

3 tablespoons boiling water, plus 1 tablespoon cold

¾ cup plain yogurt

2 tablespoons minced fresh cilantro, mint, or parsley

1 garlic clove, minced

½ teaspoon grated lemon zest plus 2 teaspoons juice

½ teaspoon table salt, divided

¼ teaspoon pepper, divided

½ teaspoon ground cumin

¼ teaspoon ground coriander

8 ounces 90 percent lean ground beef

1 tablespoon tahini

1 Combine bulgur and boiling water in large bowl; cover and let sit until bulgur is tender and all water has been absorbed, about 15 minutes.

2 Whisk yogurt, cilantro, garlic, lemon zest and juice, ¼ teaspoon salt, and ⅛ teaspoon pepper in small bowl until well combined. Stir ¼ cup yogurt mixture, cumin, coriander, remaining ¼ teaspoon salt, and remaining ⅛ teaspoon pepper into bulgur; set remaining yogurt mixture aside. Break up ground beef into small pieces over bulgur mixture and lightly knead with hands until well combined. Pinch off and roll mixture into 12 meatballs. (Meatballs and reserved yogurt mixture can be refrigerated separately for up to 24 hours.)

3 Arrange meatballs in air-fryer basket, spaced evenly apart. Place basket into air fryer and set temperature to 400 degrees. Cook until meatballs are lightly browned and register 160 degrees, 7 to 9 minutes, turning halfway through cooking.

4 Whisk tahini and cold water into reserved yogurt
mixture until smooth and sauce has consistency of heavy
cream. Adjust consistency with extra water as needed.
Serve meatballs with yogurt sauce.

Per Serving Cal 180 | Total Fat 9g | Sat Fat 3.5g | Chol 45mg | Sodium 350mg
Total Carb 10g | Dietary Fiber 2g | Total Sugars 2g | Added Sugars 0g | Protein 15g

MAKE-AHEAD CRISPY EGG ROLLS

Makes 8 egg rolls | Total Time: 50 minutes (12 minutes from frozen)

Why This Recipe Works We've all had our fair share of takeout egg rolls. They are crunchy, flavorful, and delicious, and they are usually deep-fat fried. We wanted to try frying egg rolls the air-fryer way. We prepared the filling in a skillet and then simply used the air fryer to cook the egg rolls, spritzed with a little oil, to a crisp golden. We cut down on the knife work by using bagged coleslaw mix and chose ground pork as an easy substitute for the minced fresh pork traditional recipes called for. Tasters liked the flavor of the egg rolls and loved the ability to freeze and cook them as desired. Serve the egg rolls with your favorite sauces. This recipe can be easily doubled (see page 10). The number of egg rolls you can cook at one time will depend on the size of your air fryer.

8 ounces ground pork

6 scallions, white and green parts separated and sliced thin

3 garlic cloves, minced

2 teaspoons grated fresh ginger

3 cups (7 ounces) coleslaw mix

4 ounces shiitake mushrooms, stemmed and chopped fine

2 tablespoons soy sauce

1 tablespoon sugar

1 tablespoon distilled white vinegar

2 teaspoons toasted sesame oil

8 egg roll wrappers

Canola oil spray

1 Cook pork in 12-inch nonstick skillet over medium-high heat until no longer pink, about 5 minutes, breaking up meat with spoon. Add scallion whites, garlic, and ginger and cook until fragrant, about 1 minute. Add coleslaw mix, mushrooms, soy sauce, sugar, and vinegar and cook until cabbage is just softened, about 3 minutes.

2 Off heat, stir in sesame oil and scallion greens. Transfer pork mixture to large plate; spread into even layer; and refrigerate until cool enough to handle, about 5 minutes.

3 Fill small bowl with water. Working with 1 egg roll wrapper at a time, orient wrappers on counter so 1 corner points toward edge of counter. Place lightly packed ⅓ cup filling on lower half of wrapper and mold it with your fingers into neat cylindrical shape. Using your fingertips, moisten entire border of wrapper with thin film of water.

4 Fold bottom corner of wrapper up and over filling and press it down on other side of filling. Fold both side corners of wrapper in over filling and press gently to seal. Roll filling up over itself until wrapper is fully sealed. Leave egg roll seam side down on counter and cover with damp paper towel while shaping remaining egg rolls. (Egg rolls can be refrigerated for up to 12 hours or frozen and stored in zipper-lock bag for up to 1 month. Do not thaw frozen egg rolls before cooking; increase cooking time to 12 to 18 minutes.)

5 Lightly spray air-fryer basket with oil spray. Lightly spray desired number of egg rolls with oil spray and arrange in air-fryer basket, spaced at least ½ inch apart. Place basket in air fryer and set temperature to 350 degrees. Bake until egg rolls are golden brown, 10 to 15 minutes, flipping halfway through cooking. Serve.

Per Egg Roll Cal 170 | Total Fat 8g | Sat Fat 2.5g | Chol 25mg | Sodium 390mg
Total Carb 17g | Dietary Fiber 1g | Total Sugars 3g | Added Sugars 2g | Protein 8g

MAKE-AHEAD PHYLLO HAND PIES WITH FENNEL, OLIVE, AND GOAT CHEESE FILLING

Makes 15 hand pies | Total Time: 1 hour (10 minutes from frozen)

Why This Recipe Works During testing for this book, we made a lot of sweet and savory baked goods in the air fryer. Even finicky phyllo dough, a paper-thin dough used throughout the eastern Mediterranean, is suited to its dry heat. It made the perfect parcel for little savory hand pies. Baking in a conventional oven tends to yield blond results, but our pies took on a deep golden color and turned supercrisp in the air fryer. Store-bought phyllo made it dead simple to fill, fold, and bake these triangles packed with browned fennel, meaty olives, and tangy goat cheese. Phyllo dough is also available in larger 18 by 14-inch sheets; if using, cut them in half to make 14 by 9-inch sheets. Don't thaw the phyllo in the microwave; let it sit in the refrigerator overnight or on the counter for 4 to 5 hours. This recipe can be easily doubled (see page 10). The number of hand pies you can cook at one time will depend on the size of your air fryer.

FILLING

- 1 fennel bulb, stalks discarded, bulb halved, cored, and sliced thin
- 1 tablespoon extra-virgin olive oil
- 1/8 teaspoon table salt
- 1/4 teaspoon pepper
- 1/4 cup pitted kalamata olives, chopped fine
- 2 teaspoons grated lemon zest plus 1 tablespoon juice
- 1/2 teaspoon dried oregano
- 4 ounces goat cheese, crumbled (1 cup)

HAND PIES

- 10 (14 by 9-inch) phyllo sheets, thawed
- Olive oil spray

1 FOR THE FILLING Toss fennel with oil, salt, and pepper and arrange in even layer in air-fryer basket. Set temperature to 350 degrees and cook until softened and lightly browned, 6 to 8 minutes. Transfer fennel to large bowl and stir in olives, lemon zest and juice, and oregano. Let cool completely, about 10 minutes. Stir in goat cheese gently. (Filling can be refrigerated for up to 24 hours.)

2 FOR THE HAND PIES Place one phyllo sheet on counter with long side parallel to counter edge, lightly spray with olive oil spray, then top with second phyllo sheet and lightly spray with oil spray again. Cut phyllo vertically into three 9 by 4⅔-inch strips. Place rounded 1 tablespoon of filling on bottom left-hand corner of each strip. Fold up phyllo to form right-angle triangle, pressing gently on filling as needed to create even layer. Continue folding up and over, as if folding a flag, to end of strip. Press to adhere edges.

3 Lightly spray triangle with oil spray and place seam side down on parchment paper–lined rimmed baking sheet. Repeat with remaining phyllo sheets and filling to make 15 triangles. (Hand pies can be refrigerated for up to 12 hours or frozen and stored in zipper-lock bag for up to 1 month. Do not thaw frozen hand pies before cooking; increase cooking time to 10 to 12 minutes.)

4 Lightly spray air-fryer basket with canola oil spray. Arrange desired number of hand pies in air-fryer basket, spaced at least ½ inch apart. Place basket in air fryer and set temperature to 350 degrees. Bake until hand pies are golden brown, 7 to 9 minutes, flipping halfway through cooking. Serve.

PHYLLO HAND PIES WITH APPLE, WALNUT, AND BLUE CHEESE FILLING

Combine 1 Granny Smith apple, peeled, cored, halved, and sliced thin; 3 tablespoons raisins; 1 tablespoon extra-virgin olive oil; 1½ teaspoons apple cider vinegar; 1 tablespoon water; ¼ teaspoon table salt; and ¼ teaspoon pepper in bowl. Microwave until apples begin to turn translucent and raisins are plump, about 5 minutes, stirring halfway through microwaving; let cool completely. Fold in ¼ cup chopped toasted walnuts and ½ cup crumbled blue cheese. Substitute apple filling for fennel filling.

Per Hand Pie Cal 70 | Total Fat 3.5g | Sat Fat 1.5g | Chol 5mg | Sodium 130mg
Total Carb 8g | Dietary Fiber 1g | Total Sugars 1g | Added Sugars 0g | Protein 3g

RICOTTA TARTLETS WITH TOMATO-BASIL TOPPING

Makes 12 tartlets | Total Time: 20 minutes

Why This Recipe Works These elegant and fresh little hors d'oeuvres combine the satisfying creaminess of ricotta with lightly seasoned tomato, shallot, and basil. For ease of preparation, we started with store-bought mini phyllo cups. We then mixed together some ricotta, a little olive oil, and lemon zest. After we filled the phyllo cups with our ricotta mixture, they made their way to the air fryer for a quick 5-minute bake. Not only did this allow the ricotta to set, but it also became an appetizing golden brown. Once baked, these tartlets were ready for their no-cook topping. To give you options, we also made a vibrant and crunchy topping of celery, olives, and fresh marjoram. Do not thaw the phyllo cups before baking. This recipe can be easily doubled (see page 10).

4 ounces (½ cup) part-skim ricotta

1 tablespoon extra-virgin olive oil, divided, plus extra for drizzling

1 teaspoon grated lemon zest

⅛ teaspoon table salt

⅛ teaspoon pepper

12 frozen mini phyllo cups

1 tomato, cored, seeded, and chopped

1 small shallot, minced

1 tablespoon shredded fresh basil

1 Whisk ricotta, 2 teaspoons oil, lemon zest, salt, and pepper together in bowl. Divide ricotta mixture evenly among phyllo cups, then transfer phyllo cups to air-fryer basket. Place basket into air fryer and set temperature to 300 degrees. Cook until ricotta is heated through and spotty brown, 5 to 7 minutes. Transfer to serving platter.

2 Combine tomato, shallot, basil, and remaining 1 teaspoon oil in bowl and season with salt and pepper to taste. Top tartlets with tomato mixture and drizzle with extra oil. Serve.

RICOTTA TARTLETS WITH CELERY-OLIVE TOPPING
Substitute ¼ cup minced celery for tomato, 2 tablespoons chopped pitted kalamata olives for shallot, and fresh marjoram or oregano for basil.

Per Tartlet Cal 45 | Total Fat 2.5g | Sat Fat 0.5g | Chol 5mg | Sodium 45mg
Total Carb 3g | Dietary Fiber 0g | Total Sugars 1g | Added Sugars 0g | Protein 2g

ASPARAGUS FRIES WITH YOGURT SAUCE

Serves 2 | Total Time: 30 minutes

Why This Recipe Works In the spring, asparagus is plentiful, and we like to cook it in myriad ways. Here we air-fry this sweet, grassy vegetable and turn it into fries for a deliciously quick and easy appetizer or side. A combination of toasted panko bread crumbs and grated Parmesan gave a delightfully crackly and delicate exterior to the asparagus. To make the panko mixture stick to the vegetable, we used a combination of flour and egg seasoned with herbes de Provence, salt, and pepper. Arranging the coated asparagus pieces in a "Lincoln Log" pattern (see page 5) in the basket allowed for maximum air circulation. Look for asparagus that is approximately ½ inch at the base.

- ½ cup plain yogurt
- 1 tablespoon whole-grain mustard
- ¾ cup panko bread crumbs
- 2 tablespoons extra-virgin olive oil

- 1 ounce Parmesan cheese, grated (½ cup)
- 1 large egg
- 1 tablespoon all-purpose flour
- ½ teaspoon herbes de Provence

- ½ teaspoon table salt
- ¼ teaspoon pepper
- 1 pound asparagus, trimmed and halved crosswise
- Lemon wedges

1 Whisk yogurt and mustard together in small bowl; set aside for serving. Toss panko with oil in shallow dish until evenly coated. Microwave, stirring frequently, until light golden brown, 1 to 3 minutes. Let cool slightly, then stir in Parmesan. Whisk egg, flour, herbes de Provence, salt, and pepper together in second shallow dish. Working with several asparagus pieces at a time, dredge in egg mixture, letting excess drip off, then coat with panko mixture, pressing gently to adhere; transfer to large plate.

2 Lightly spray base of air-fryer basket with canola oil spray. Arrange half of asparagus pieces parallel to each other in prepared basket, spaced evenly apart. Arrange remaining asparagus pieces on top, perpendicular to first layer. Place basket into air fryer and set temperature to 400 degrees. Cook until asparagus are tender and crisp, 10 to 12 minutes, shaking basket gently to loosen pieces halfway through cooking. Serve with yogurt sauce and lemon wedges.

Per Serving Cal 200 | Total Fat 11g | Sat Fat 2.5g | Chol 45mg | Sodium 510mg
Total Carb 16g | Dietary Fiber 1g | Total Sugars 3g | Added Sugars 0g | Protein 8g

SHOESTRING FRIES

Serves 2 | Total Time: 45 minutes

Why This Recipe Works In the realm of fries, the flavor of shoestring fries is hard to beat. Their thinner shape allows for more of our favorite part—the crunch. Instead of cutting them by hand, we used a spiralizer to quickly cut potatoes into thin, even strings. Then we cut them into manageable 4-inch lengths. This was followed by rinsing to remove excess starch and a thorough drying with paper towels. We coated the fries with just 2 tablespoons of oil, which made them perfectly golden while still maintaining a dry, crisp exterior. To mix up the flavor, try one of our seasoning variations. Serve these fries with your favorite dipping sauce. We found that frequently tossing the potatoes ensured the most even cooking and the best browning. You will need a spiralizer with a ¼-inch (6mm) noodle attachment for this recipe.

1 pound russet potatoes, unpeeled

2 tablespoons canola oil

¼ teaspoon table salt

⅛ teaspoon pepper

1 Use chef's knife to trim off ends of potatoes. Using spiralizer fitted with ¼-inch (6mm) noodle attachment, cut potatoes into ribbons, cutting ribbons into 4-inch lengths with kitchen shears as you spiralize. Submerge potatoes in large bowl of water and rinse to remove excess starch. Drain potatoes and repeat process as needed until water remains clear. Drain potatoes, transfer to paper towel–lined rimmed baking sheet, and thoroughly pat dry.

2 Toss potatoes with oil, salt, and pepper. Arrange potatoes in even layer in air-fryer basket. Place basket into air fryer and set temperature to 350 degrees. Cook for 15 to 20 minutes, using tongs to toss gently and separate potatoes every 5 minutes to prevent sticking. Season with salt and pepper to taste, and serve.

SHOESTRING FRIES WITH ROSEMARY AND LEMON ZEST
Sprinkle 1 teaspoon minced fresh rosemary over potatoes and toss to combine before final 5 minutes of cooking. Before serving, toss fries with 1 teaspoon grated lemon zest.

SHOESTRING FRIES WITH CORIANDER AND DILL
Sprinkle 1 teaspoon ground coriander and ½ teaspoon pepper over potatoes and toss to combine before final 5 minutes of cooking. Before serving, toss fries with 1 teaspoon minced fresh dill.

Per Serving Cal 150 | Total Fat 7g | Sat Fat 1g | Chol 0mg | Sodium 150mg
Total Carb 20g | Dietary Fiber 1g | Total Sugars 1g | Added Sugars 0g | Protein 2g

WHOLE-WHEAT PITA CHIPS WITH SALT AND PEPPER

Serves 2 (makes 16 chips) | Total Time: 20 minutes, plus 30 minutes cooling

Why This Recipe Works Store-bought pita chips are tasty but homemade chips are more flavorful and fresh, and they're easy to make. We chose to use whole-wheat pita and separated an 8-inch round into its two component layers. We sprayed the split rounds with olive oil and seasoned them with salt and pepper before cutting them into wedges—much easier than spraying and seasoning each individual wedge. In a traditional oven, we would arrange the pita wedges in a single layer on a baking sheet to facilitate even cooking, but the gently circulating heat within the air fryer meant that we could pile the wedges into two layers that would cook quickly and evenly in the compact space; we tossed them once halfway through cooking. We loved the elegant simplicity of chips seasoned with salt and pepper, but we also developed two flavor variations—tangy buttermilk-ranch chips and warmly spiced ras el hanout chips—to jazz up the snack table. Traditional pita also works well here. This recipe can be easily doubled (see page 10).

1 (8-inch) 100-percent whole-wheat pita

Olive oil spray

⅛ teaspoon table salt

⅛ teaspoon pepper

1 Using kitchen shears, cut around perimeter of pita and separate into 2 thin rounds. Lightly spray both sides of each cut round with oil spray and sprinkle with salt and pepper. Cut each round into 8 wedges.

2 Arrange wedges into two even layers in air-fryer basket. Place basket into air fryer and set temperature to 300 degrees. Cook until wedges are light golden brown on edges, 3 to 5 minutes. Using tongs, toss wedges gently to redistribute and continue to cook until golden brown and crisp, 3 to 5 minutes. Let cool completely, about 30 minutes, before serving. (Chips can be stored in airtight container for up to 3 days.)

BUTTERMILK-RANCH WHOLE-WHEAT PITA CHIPS

Omit salt and pepper. Sprinkle each oiled pita round with ½ teaspoon buttermilk-ranch seasoning powder before cutting into wedges.

RAS EL HANOUT WHOLE-WHEAT PITA CHIPS

Omit pepper. Sprinkle each oiled pita round with ¼ teaspoon ras el hanout before cutting into wedges.

Per Serving Cal 70 | Total Fat 1g | Sat Fat 0g | Chol 0mg | Sodium 260mg
Total Carb 14g | Dietary Fiber 0g | Total Sugars 1g | Added Sugars 0g | Protein 4g

ROMESCO

Makes about 1½ cups | Total Time: 40 minutes

Why This Recipe Works Wanting to see how far we could go with using the air fryer to cook different ingredients, we made romesco, a classic Catalan sauce from the Spanish province of Tarragona. Traditionally used as a spread; an accompaniment to meats, fish, or vegetables; or the base of a stew, we put romesco, a sweet, tangy combination of dried ñora chiles, roasted tomatoes, garlic, toasted nuts, bread, olive oil, and vinegar, to use as a dip. We rehydrated dried ñora chiles in hot water. Meanwhile, we used the air fryer to roast tomatoes until lightly browned, toast bread and nuts, and roast garlic cloves, too. Then we processed the cooked ingredients with the rehydrated chiles, water, olive oil, and vinegar to create an earthy, creamy sauce. You can substitute ancho chiles for ñoras. This recipe can be easily doubled (see page 10). Serve with toasted baguette slices, pita chips, crackers, and/or crudités.

1 ounce dried ñora or ancho chiles, stemmed and seeded

1 (3-inch) piece baguette (1½ ounces), cut into 4 slices

¼ cup whole blanched hazelnuts and/or almonds

6 garlic cloves, lightly crushed and peeled

2 tablespoons extra-virgin olive oil, divided, plus extra for serving

6 plum tomatoes, cored and halved lengthwise

1 tablespoon sherry or red wine vinegar, plus extra for seasoning

½ teaspoon table salt

1 Place ñoras in bowl; cover with hot water; and let sit until softened, 20 to 30 minutes. Drain chiles and discard soaking liquid. Meanwhile, toss baguette slices, hazelnuts, and garlic with 1 tablespoon oil.

2. Arrange tomatoes cut side up in air-fryer basket. Place basket into air fryer; set temperature to 400 degrees; and cook until tomatoes are spotty brown, skins are blistered, and tomatoes have begun to collapse, 12 to 18 minutes. Arrange bread, hazelnuts, and garlic around tomatoes in air-fryer basket and cook until bread, hazelnuts, and garlic are deep golden brown and tomatoes are well browned, 5 to 7 minutes.

3 Transfer tomato-bread mixture to food-processor bowl and add ñoras and salt. Pulse until mixture is coarsely ground, 6 to 8 pulses, scraping down sides of bowl as needed. Add 3 tablespoons water, vinegar, and remaining 1 tablespoon oil and process until mixture is mostly smooth, about 2 minutes. (Add up to ¼ cup extra water, 1 tablespoon at a time, as needed to achieve consistency of thick mayonnaise.) Season romesco with salt, pepper, and extra vinegar to taste. Transfer to serving bowl and drizzle with extra oil. Serve. (Romesco can be refrigerated for up to 2 days; bring to room temperature and whisk to recombine before serving.)

Per ¼-Cup Serving Cal 130 | Total Fat 9g | Sat Fat 1g | Chol 0mg | Sodium 240mg
Total Carb 10g | Dietary Fiber 3g | Total Sugars 2g | Added Sugars 0g | Protein 3g

CRISPY BARBECUE CHICKPEAS

Makes about 1 cup | Total Time: 45 minutes

Why This Recipe Works Wait till you get your hands on these crispy, pantry-friendly chickpeas. The air fryer transforms soft and creamy canned chickpeas into crisp, golden-brown, nutty bites of protein goodness. We discovered that we could streamline the cooking method of our successful oven-roasted chickpeas, which requires the chickpeas to first dry out in the microwave. The air-fryer method allowed us to omit the microwaving step because the dry heat of the air fryer dries out the chickpeas, allowing them to split open, release their interior steam, and get perfectly crisp in about 30 minutes. Coating them in extra-virgin olive oil allowed the legumes to develop a deep golden-brown hue. We tossed the chickpeas with the spice blends after the crisping process so that the spices didn't burn in the air fryer. The heat from the chickpeas was enough to successfully "bloom" the spices. This recipe can be easily doubled (see page 10).

- 1 (15-ounce) can chickpeas
- 4 teaspoons extra-virgin olive oil
- 1½ teaspoons chili powder
- ¾ teaspoon sugar
- ½ teaspoon garlic powder
- Pinch table salt
- Pinch cayenne pepper

1 Drain chickpeas thoroughly (do not rinse), then pat dry with paper towels. Toss chickpeas with oil until evenly coated, then transfer to air-fryer basket and spread into single layer. Place basket into air fryer and set temperature to 300 degrees. Cook until chickpeas appear dry, slightly shriveled, and deep golden brown, 25 to 35 minutes, tossing occasionally. (To test for doneness, remove a few paler chickpeas and let cool briefly before tasting; if interiors are soft, return to air fryer for 2 minutes before testing again.)

2 Combine chili powder, sugar, garlic powder, salt, and cayenne in large bowl. Add chickpeas and toss to coat. Let cool completely before serving, about 10 minutes. (Chickpeas can be stored in airtight container for up to 1 week.)

CRISPY CORIANDER-CUMIN CHICKPEAS
Reduce sugar to ¼ teaspoon. Substitute ½ teaspoon ground coriander, ¼ teaspoon ground turmeric, and ¼ teaspoon ground cumin for chili powder and garlic powder.

CRISPY SMOKED PAPRIKA CHICKPEAS
Reduce sugar to ¼ teaspoon. Substitute 1½ teaspoons smoked paprika and ¼ teaspoon onion powder for chili powder and garlic powder.

Per ¼-Cup Serving Cal 110 | Total Fat 6g | Sat Fat 1g | Chol 0mg | Sodium 230mg
Total Carb 11g | Dietary Fiber 3g | Total Sugars 1g | Added Sugars 1g | Protein 4g

DATE-ALMOND SNACK BARS

Makes 8 bars | Total Time: 1 hour, plus 1 hour cooling

Why This Recipe Works To make a delicious and nutritious snack (or breakfast) bar packed with protein and fiber, we first toasted a collection of nuts and seeds in a cake pan. A blitzed mix of dates and a touch of maple syrup helped hold everything together when we pressed the mixture back in the same cake pan. Lining the pan with foil made it easy to get the bars in and out. The result was evenly toasted wedges with good crunch and a slight chew. Use pure maple syrup, not pancake syrup, here. You will need a 6-inch round nonstick or silicone cake pan for this recipe; before starting this recipe, confirm your air fryer allows enough space for the pan.

⅔ cup whole raw almonds, cashews, pecans, and/or walnuts

5 tablespoons raw pepitas and/or sunflower seeds

2 tablespoons whole flax seeds and/or sesame seeds

3 ounces pitted dates

2 tablespoons warm water

1 tablespoon maple syrup

1 teaspoon grated orange zest

¼ teaspoon table salt

⅛ teaspoon ground cinnamon

1 Combine almonds, pepitas, and flax seeds in 6-inch nonstick round cake pan. Place pan in air-fryer basket. Place basket into air fryer; set temperature to 350 degrees; and cook until nuts and seeds are toasted and fragrant, 3 to 5 minutes, stirring halfway through cooking.

2 Transfer nut mixture to food processor and let cool slightly; reserve pan. Process nut mixture until ground medium-fine, 15 to 20 seconds; transfer to large bowl. Process dates, warm water, maple syrup, orange zest, salt, and cinnamon in now-empty processor until finely chopped, scraping down sides of bowl as needed, about 30 seconds. Stir date mixture into nut mixture, folding and pressing with rubber spatula, until well combined.

3 Line now-empty pan with aluminum foil, pressing foil into corners of pan, and lightly spray with vegetable oil spray. Transfer mixture to prepared pan and press firmly into even layer with greased spatula. Return pan to air-fryer basket and return basket to air fryer. Set temperature to 300 degrees and cook until bars are evenly browned, 14 to 20 minutes.

4 Let bars cool in pan for 15 minutes. Using foil sling, remove bars from pan and transfer to wire rack. Discard foil and let bars cool completely, about 1 hour. Cut bars into 8 wedges and serve. (Bars can be stored in airtight container for up to 1 week.)

Per Bar Cal 140 | Total Fat 9g | Sat Fat 1g | Chol 0mg | Sodium 40mg
Total Carb 13g | Dietary Fiber 3g | Total Sugars 9g | Added Sugars 2g | Protein 5g

ALMOND, CHERRY, AND CHOCOLATE TRAIL MIX

Serves 6 to 8 (makes 4 cups) | Total Time: 35 minutes, plus 1 hour cooling

Why This Recipe Works The combination of oats, almonds, coconut, and crisp pepitas in this snack mix forms a pretty healthy base for the add-ins of dried cherries and dark chocolate. To tie everything together, we seasoned our mix with vanilla and allspice, plus a touch of salt to elevate the flavors. Store-bought trail mixes are often packed with sugar, but we were satisfied with a moderate amount of maple syrup, which helped to bind our oats and create clusters. We found that moving the oat mixture around during cooking caused small bits to fall through the basket, whereas a longer cooking time at a lower temperature produced an even, golden-brown color without stirring. Use pure maple syrup, not pancake syrup, here. You can substitute pistachios, cashews, walnuts, peanuts, or hazelnuts for the almonds and dried cranberries for the cherries. Do not substitute quick oats, instant oats, or steel-cut oats in this recipe. Make sure that the oat-nut mixture has cooled completely before adding the cherries and chocolate. This recipe can be easily doubled (see page 10).

- 3 tablespoons maple syrup
- 1 tablespoon extra-virgin olive oil
- 1 teaspoon vanilla extract
- ¼ teaspoon ground allspice
- ¼ teaspoon table salt
- 1½ cups (4½ ounces) old-fashioned rolled oats
- ½ cup whole almonds
- ½ cup unsweetened flaked coconut
- ¼ cup raw pepitas
- ½ cup unsweetened dried cherries
- 4 ounces bittersweet chocolate, chopped coarse

1 Lightly spray air-fryer basket with vegetable oil spray. Whisk maple syrup, oil, vanilla, allspice, and salt together in large bowl. Stir in oats, almonds, coconut, and pepitas until all ingredients are evenly moistened. Scrape oat mixture into prepared basket and spread into even layer. Place basket into air fryer; set temperature to 300 degrees; and cook, without stirring, until oat-almond mixture is golden brown, 14 to 20 minutes.

2 Remove basket from air fryer and let oat-almond mixture cool completely, about 1 hour. Transfer mixture to clean large bowl, breaking up larger clusters, and stir in cherries and chocolate. Serve. (Trail mix can be stored in airtight container for up to 2 weeks.)

Per ½-Cup Serving Cal 240 | Total Fat 14g | Sat Fat 5g | Chol 0mg | Sodium 65mg
Total Carb 26g | Dietary Fiber 4g | Total Sugars 7g | Added Sugars 4g | Protein 5g

CONVERSIONS AND EQUIVALENTS

Some say cooking is a science and an art. We would say that geography has a hand in it, too. Flours and sugars manufactured in the United Kingdom and elsewhere will feel and taste different from those manufactured in the United States. So we cannot promise that the loaf of bread you bake in Canada or England will taste the same as a loaf baked in the States, but we can offer guidelines for converting weights and measures. We also recommend that you rely on your instincts when making our recipes. Refer to the visual cues provided.

The recipes in this book were developed using standard U.S. measures following U.S. government guidelines. The charts below offer equivalents for U.S. and metric measures. All conversions are approximate and have been rounded up or down to the nearest whole number.

Example

1 teaspoon	=	4.9292 milliliters, rounded up to 5 milliliters
1 ounce	=	28.3495 grams, rounded down to 28 grams

Converting Fahrenheit to Celsius

We include temperatures in some of the recipes in this book and we recommend an instant-read thermometer for the job. To convert Fahrenheit degrees to Celsius, use this simple formula:

Subtract 32 degrees from the Fahrenheit reading, then divide the result by 1.8 to find the Celsius reading. For example, to convert 160°F to Celsius:

$$160°F - 32 = 128°$$
$$128° \div 1.8 = 71.11°C$$
rounded down to 71°C

Volume Conversions

U.S.	METRIC
1 teaspoon	5 milliliters
2 teaspoons	10 milliliters
1 tablespoon	15 milliliters
2 tablespoons	30 milliliters
¼ cup	59 milliliters
⅓ cup	79 milliliters
½ cup	118 milliliters
¾ cup	177 milliliters
1 cup	237 milliliters
1¼ cups	296 milliliters
1½ cups	355 milliliters
2 cups (1 pint)	473 milliliters
2½ cups	591 milliliters
3 cups	710 milliliters
4 cups (1 quart)	0.946 liter
1.06 quarts	1 liter
4 quarts (1 gallon)	3.8 liters

Weight Conversions

OUNCES	GRAMS
½	14
¾	21
1	28
1½	43
2	57
2½	71
3	85
3½	99
4	113
4½	128
5	142
6	170
7	198
8	227
9	255
10	283
12	340
16 (1 pound)	454

INDEX

Note: Page references in *italics* indicate photographs

A

Air fryers
arranging skewers in, 5
attachments, note about, 5
drawer-style, 6, 8–9
equipment to use with, 11
Instant Pot lid for, 6
making foil sling for, 5
oven-style, 7, 9
ratings of, 8–9
scaling recipes for, 10
simple uses for, 12–13
styles of, 6–7
ten ways to eat healthy with, 2–3
tips and techniques for success, 5
Almond Butter and Roasted Fruit Toast, 28, *29*
Almond(s)
-Blueberry Muffins, Whole-Wheat, *34,* 35
Cherry, and Chocolate Trail Mix, 174, *175*
Currant, and Oat Scones with Earl Grey Glaze, 33
-Date Snack Bars, *172,* 173
Dried Cherries, and Balsamic Vinaigrette, Roasted Leeks with, 136, *137*
Romesco, *168,* 169
Smoked, –Crusted Salmon, 97
Aluminum foil, 11
muffin-tin liners, 11
slings, preparing, 5
Apple
Crisp, 13, *13*
-Fennel Salad, Creamy, Crispy Breaded Chicken Breasts with, 42–43, *43*
Walnut, and Blue Cheese Filling, Phyllo Hand Pies with, 159
Apricot, Pistachio, and Oat Scones with Garam Masala Glaze, 33
Artichokes, Spinach, and Feta, Baked Eggs with, 20, *21*

B

Asparagus
and Citrus Salad, Roasted Swordfish with, 108–9, *109*
Fries with Yogurt Sauce, 162, *163*

Bean(s)
Black, and Corn Salad, Flank Steak with, *80,* 81
Cannellini, and Watercress, Spicy Roasted Shrimp and Fennel Salad with, 112–13, *113*
Chicken and Chickpea Salad with Carrots, Cucumber, and Feta, *60,* 61
Crispy Barbecue Chickpeas, 170, *171*
Crispy Coriander-Cumin Chickpeas, 170
Crispy Smoked Paprika Chickpeas, 170
Green, and Hazelnuts, Lemon-Thyme Pork Tenderloin with, 90–91, *91*
Green, Charred, and Tomatoes, Spicy Peanut Chicken with, 48–49, *49*
Make-Ahead Breakfast Burritos, 24–25, *25*
White, and Mushroom Gratin, 122–23, *123*
Beef
-and-Bulgur Meatballs with Tahini-Yogurt Dipping Sauce, 154–55, *155*
Flank Steak with Corn and Black Bean Salad, *80,* 81
Lemon-Sage Top Sirloin Steak with Roasted Carrots and Shallots, *74,* 75
Roasted Steak Tips with Tomatoes and Gorgonzola, 72, *73*
Steak Frites, 78–79, *79*
Top Sirloin Steak with Roasted Zucchini and Shiitakes, 76–77, *77*
Blackberry, Roasted Peach, and Arugula Salad, Crispy Pork Chops with, 84–85, *85*
Blueberry-Almond Muffins, Whole-Wheat, *34,* 35
Bok Choy, Sesame, Sweet and Spicy Glazed Pork Chops with, 86–87, *87*

Bread
Egg in a Hole with Tomato, Avocado, and Herb Salad, 16, *17*
Roasted Fruit and Almond Butter Toast, 28, *29*
Zucchini, and Red Pepper Hash, Smoky, Baked Eggs with, *18,* 19
see also Pita Chips
Broccoli
Kimchi, and Shiitakes, Roasted, Sesame Salmon with, *100,* 101
Roasted, *130,* 131
Roasted, with Parmesan, Lemon, and Black Pepper Topping, 131
Roasted, with Sesame and Lime Topping, 131
Sun-Dried Tomato, and Cheddar Frittata, 23
Brussels Sprout(s)
and Citrus Salad, Chipotle-Honey Fried Chicken with, 50–51, *51*
and Leek, Harissa-Rubbed Haddock with, *104,* 105
Bulgur
-and-Beef Meatballs with Tahini-Yogurt Dipping Sauce, 154–55, *155*
Make-Ahead Lentil and Mushroom Burgers, 128–29, *129*
Make-Ahead Lentil and Mushroom Burgers with Radicchio and Pear Salad, 129
and Vegetable Salad, Spiced Chicken Kebabs with, 58–59, *59*
Burgers
California Turkey, *40,* 41
Lentil and Mushroom, Make-Ahead, 128–29, *129*
Lentil and Mushroom, Make-Ahead, with Radicchio and Pear Salad, 129
Salmon, with Tomato Chutney, 102–3, *103*
Burritos, Make-Ahead Breakfast, 24–25, *25*

C

Cabbage

Make-Ahead Crispy Egg Rolls, 156–57, *157*

Napa, Shiitakes, and Bell Pepper, Hoisin-Ginger Chicken Salad with, 62–63, *63*

Cake pans, 11

Cakes, Warm Chocolate Fudge, 13, *13*

Cantaloupe-Cucumber Salad, Prosciutto-Wrapped Chicken with, *44*, 45

Carrots

Cucumber, and Feta, Chicken and Chickpea Salad with, *60*, 61

and Shallots, Roasted, Lemon-Sage Top Sirloin Steak with, *74*, 75

Cauliflower and Shallots, Roasted, Coriander Chicken Thighs with, 56–57, *57*

Celery-Olive Topping, Ricotta Tartlets with, 161

Cheese

Asparagus Fries with Yogurt Sauce, 162, *163*

Baked Eggs with Spinach, Artichokes, and Feta, 20, *21*

Blue, Apple, and Walnut Filling, Phyllo Hand Pies with, 159

Broccoli, Sun-Dried Tomato, and Cheddar Frittata, 23

California Turkey Burgers, *40*, 41

Chicken and Chickpea Salad with Carrots, Cucumber, and Feta, *60*, 61

Goat, and Chive Sauce, 147

Goat, Fennel, and Olive Filling, Make-Ahead Phyllo Hand Pies with, 158–59, *159*

Goat, Kale, and Roasted Red Pepper Frittata, *22*, 23

Parmesan-Garlic Chicken Wings, 150

Prosciutto-Wrapped Chicken with Cantaloupe-Cucumber Salad, *44*, 45

Ricotta Tartlets with Celery-Olive Topping, 161

Cheese (*cont.*)

Ricotta Tartlets with Tomato-Basil Topping, *160*, 161

Roasted Broccoli with Parmesan, Lemon, and Black Pepper Topping, 131

Roasted Butternut Squash Salad with Za'atar and Halloumi, *124*, 125

Roasted Steak Tips with Tomatoes and Gorgonzola, 72, *73*

Swiss, Ham, and Pea Frittata, 23

Turkey-Zucchini Meatballs with Orzo, Spiced Tomato Sauce, and Feta, 38–39, *39*

Cherry(ies)

Almond, and Chocolate Trail Mix, 174, *175*

Dried, Almonds, and Balsamic Vinaigrette, Roasted Leeks with, 136, *137*

Chicken

Breast, Brown Sugar–Balsamic-Glazed Bone-In, 46, *47*

Breast, Honey-Miso-Glazed Bone-In, 46

Breast, Peach-Jalapeño-Glazed Bone-In, 46

Breasts, Crispy Breaded, with Creamy Apple-Fennel Salad, 42–43, *43*

and Chickpea Salad with Carrots, Cucumber, and Feta, *60*, 61

Chipotle-Honey Fried, with Brussels Sprout and Citrus Salad, 50–51, *51*

Kebabs, Red Curry, with Peanut Dipping Sauce, *152*, 153

Kebabs, Spiced, with Vegetable and Bulgur Salad, 58–59, *59*

Prosciutto-Wrapped, with Cantaloupe-Cucumber Salad, *44*, 45

Salad, Hoisin-Ginger, with Napa Cabbage, Shiitakes, and Bell Pepper, 62–63, *63*

Spicy Peanut, with Charred Green Beans and Tomatoes, 48–49, *49*

Thighs, Coriander, with Roasted Cauliflower and Shallots, 56–57, *57*

Thighs, Roasted, with Potatoes and Mesclun Salad, 52–53, *53*

Chicken (*cont.*)

Thighs with Roasted Mushrooms and Tomatoes, *54*, 55

-Tomatillo Tacos with Roasted Pineapple Salsa, 64–65, *65*

Whole Roast, with Ginger, Cumin, and Cardamom, 69

Whole Roast, with Lemon, Dill, and Garlic, 68–69, *69*

Whole Roast, with Orange, Aleppo, and Cinnamon, 69

Wings, Cilantro-Lime, 150

Wings, Lemon-Pepper, 150, *151*

Wings, Parmesan-Garlic, 150

Chicken Sausages, Roasted, with Butternut Squash and Radicchio, *66*, 67

Chiles, toasting, 12

Chocolate

Almond, and Cherry Trail Mix, 174, *175*

Fudge Cakes, Warm, 13, *13*

Cilantro-Lime Chicken Wings, 150

Citrus

and Asparagus Salad, Roasted Swordfish with, 108–9, *109*

and Brussels Sprout Salad, Chipotle-Honey Fried Chicken with, 50–51, *51*

see also Orange(s)

Corn

and Black Bean Salad, Flank Steak with, *80*, 81

Kale, and Pickled Jalapeños, Stuffed Portobello Mushrooms with, 120–21, *121*

Cucumber(s)

-Cantaloupe Salad, Prosciutto-Wrapped Chicken with, *44*, 45

Carrots, and Feta, Chicken and Chickpea Salad with, *60*, 61

and Mango Salad, Ginger-Turmeric Scallops with, 110–11, *111*

Currant, Almond, and Oat Scones with Earl Grey Glaze, 33

D

Date-Almond Snack Bars, *172*, 173
Desserts
Apple Crisp, 13, *13*
Warm Chocolate Fudge Cakes, 13, *13*

E

Eggplant
Roasted, with Capers, Oregano, and
Garlic, 132, *133*
and Five-Spice Tofu, Ramen Noodle Bowl
with, 126–27, *127*
Egg Rolls, Make-Ahead Crispy, 156–57, *157*
Egg(s)
Baked, with Smoky Zucchini, Red Pepper,
and Bread Hash, *18*, 19
Baked, with Spinach, Artichokes, and
Feta, 20, *21*
in a Hole with Tomato, Avocado, and Herb
Salad, 16, *17*
Make-Ahead Breakfast Burritos, 24–25, *25*
see also Frittatas
Equipment, 11

F

Fennel
-Apple Salad, Creamy, Crispy Breaded
Chicken Breasts with, 42–43, *43*
Olive, and Goat Cheese Filling, Make-
Ahead Phyllo Hand Pies with,
158–59, *159*
Roasted, with Orange-Honey Dressing,
134, 135
and Shrimp, Spicy Roasted, Salad with
Cannellini Beans and Watercress,
112–13, *113*
Fish
Crispy Halibut with Leafy Greens and
Tartar Sauce, 106–7, *107*
Harissa-Rubbed Haddock with Brussels
Sprouts and Leek, *104*, 105

Fish (*cont.*)
Roasted Swordfish with Asparagus and
Citrus Salad, 108–9, *109*
see also Salmon
Fish spatula, 11
Fries
Asparagus, with Yogurt Sauce, 162, *163*
Shoestring, *164*, 165
Shoestring, with Coriander and Dill, 165
Shoestring, with Rosemary and Lemon
Zest, 165
Frittatas
Broccoli, Sun-Dried Tomato, and
Cheddar, 23
Ham, Pea, and Swiss Cheese, 23
Kale, Roasted Red Pepper, and Goat
Cheese, *22*, 23
Fruit
Oat, and Nut Scones, Make-Ahead, 32, *33*
Roasted, and Almond Butter Toast, 28, *29*
Roasted, Topping, 12
see also specific fruits

G

Garlic, Roasted, 12
Grain(s)
Bowl, Overnight Breakfast, *30*, 31
Three-, Bowl, Overnight Breakfast, 31
see also specific grains
Green Beans
Charred, and Tomatoes, Spicy Peanut
Chicken with, 48–49, *49*
and Hazelnuts, Lemon-Thyme Pork
Tenderloin with, 90–91, *91*
Greens
Leafy, and Tartar Sauce, Crispy Halibut
with, 106–7, *107*
see also specific greens
Gyros, Marinated Pork, 92–93, *93*

H

Haddock, Harissa-Rubbed, with Brussels
Sprouts and Leek, *104*, 105
Halibut, Crispy, with Leafy Greens and
Tartar Sauce, 106–7, *107*
Ham
Pea, and Swiss Cheese Frittata, 23
Prosciutto-Wrapped Chicken with
Cantaloupe-Cucumber Salad, *44*, 45
Hand Pies
Make-Ahead Phyllo, with Fennel, Olive,
and Goat Cheese Filling, 158–59, *159*
Phyllo, with Apple, Walnut, and Blue
Cheese Filling, 159
Hash, Hearty Vegetable, with Golden
Yogurt, *26*, 27
Hazelnut(s)
-Crusted Salmon, 97
and Green Beans, Lemon-Thyme Pork
Tenderloin with, 90–91, *91*
Romesco, *168*, 169
Hoisin
-Ginger Chicken Salad with Napa Cabbage,
Shiitakes, and Bell Pepper, 62–63, *63*
Spicy Peanut Chicken with Charred Green
Beans and Tomatoes, 48–49, *49*

K

Kale
Corn, and Pickled Jalapeños, Stuffed
Portobello Mushrooms with, 120–21, *121*
Hearty Vegetable Hash with Golden
Yogurt, *26*, 27
Make-Ahead Breakfast Burritos, 24–25, *25*
Roasted Red Pepper, and Goat Cheese
Frittata, *22*, 23
Kebabs
Red Curry Chicken, with Peanut Dipping
Sauce, *152*, 153
Spiced Chicken, with Vegetable and
Bulgur Salad, 58–59, *59*
Kimchi, Broccoli, and Shiitakes, Roasted,
Sesame Salmon with, *100*, 101

L

Leek(s)

and Brussels Sprouts, Harissa-Rubbed
Haddock with, *104, 105*

Roasted, with Almonds, Dried Cherries,
and Balsamic Vinaigrette, 136, *137*

Lentil

and Mushroom Burgers, Make-Ahead,
128–29, *129*

and Mushroom Burgers, Make-Ahead, with
Radicchio and Pear Salad, 129

M

Make-Ahead Breakfast Burritos, 24–25, *25*

Make-Ahead Crispy Egg Rolls, 156–57, *157*

Make-Ahead Fruit, Nut, and Oat Scones,
32, *33*

Make-Ahead Lentil and Mushroom Burgers,
128–29, *129*

Make-Ahead Lentil and Mushroom Burgers
with Radicchio and Pear Salad, 129

Make-Ahead Phyllo Hand Pies with
Fennel, Olive, and Goat Cheese Filling,
158–59, *159*

Mango and Cucumber Salad, Ginger-
Turmeric Scallops with, 110–11, *111*

Maple Syrup, Spicy, 147

Meatballs

Beef-and-Bulgur, with Tahini-Yogurt
Dipping Sauce, 154–55, *155*

Turkey-Zucchini, with Orzo, Spiced
Tomato Sauce, and Feta, 38–39, *39*

Mesclun Salad and Potatoes, Roasted
Chicken Thighs with, 52–53, *53*

Miso-Honey-Glazed Bone-In Chicken
Breast, 46

Muffins

liners and cups for, 11

Whole-Wheat Blueberry-Almond,
34, 35

Mushroom(s)

Hearty Vegetable Hash with Golden
Yogurt, *26,* 27

Hoisin-Ginger Chicken Salad with Napa
Cabbage, Shiitakes, and Bell Pepper,
62–63, *63*

and Lentil Burgers, Make-Ahead,
128–29, *129*

and Lentil Burgers, Make-Ahead, with
Radicchio and Pear Salad, 129

Roasted, with Shallot and Thyme, *138,* 139

Sesame Salmon with Roasted Kimchi,
Broccoli, and Shiitakes, *100,* 101

Stuffed Portobello, with Kale, Corn, and
Pickled Jalapeños, 120–21, *121*

and Tomatoes, Roasted, Chicken Thighs
with, *54,* 55

Top Sirloin Steak with Roasted Zucchini
and Shiitakes, 76–77, *77*

and White Bean Gratin, 122–23, *123*

N

Noodle(s)

Curry, Shrimp with, 114–15, *115*

Ramen, Bowl with Eggplant and Five-
Spice Tofu, 126–27, *127*

Nut(s)

Oat, and Fruit Scones, Make-Ahead, 32, *33*

toasting, 12

see also specific nuts

O

Oat(s)

Almond, Cherry, and Chocolate Trail Mix,
174, 175

Apricot, and Pistachio Scones with Garam
Masala Glaze, 33

Currant, and Almond Scones with Earl
Grey Glaze, 33

Fruit, and Nut Scones, Make-Ahead, 32, *33*

Oil mister, 11

Olive

-Celery Topping, Ricotta Tartlets with, 161

Fennel, and Goat Cheese Filling, Make-
Ahead Phyllo Hand Pies with,
158–59, *159*

Orange(s)

Aleppo, and Cinnamon, Whole Roast
Chicken with, 69

Chipotle-Honey Fried Chicken with
Brussels Sprout and Citrus Salad,
50–51, *51*

-Honey Dressing, Roasted Fennel with,
134, 135

Roasted Swordfish with Asparagus and
Citrus Salad, 108–9, *109*

**Orzo, Spiced Tomato Sauce, and Feta,
Turkey-Zucchini Meatballs with,
38–39, *39***

Oven mitts, 11

Ovensafe bowl, 11

P

Parsley-Shallot Sauce, 78, *79*

Pasta. *See* Orzo

Peach

-Jalapeño-Glazed Bone-In Chicken
Breast, 46

Roasted, Blackberry, and Arugula Salad,
Crispy Pork Chops with, 84–85, *85*

Peanut butter

Red Curry Chicken Kebabs with Peanut
Dipping Sauce, *152,* 153

Spicy Peanut Chicken with Charred Green
Beans and Tomatoes, 48–49, *49*

**Pear and Radicchio Salad, Make-Ahead
Lentil and Mushroom Burgers with, 129**

Pea(s)

Ham, and Swiss Cheese Frittata, 23

Snap, and Radishes, Honey-Glazed
Salmon with, 98–99, *99*

Pepper(s)

Bell, Napa Cabbage, and Shiitakes, Hoisin-
Ginger Chicken Salad with, 62–63, *63*

Pepper(s) (*cont.*)

Red, Zucchini, and Bread Hash, Smoky, Baked Eggs with, *18,* 19

Roasted Red, Kale, and Goat Cheese Frittata, *22, 23*

toasting chiles, 12

Phyllo

Hand Pies, Make-Ahead, with Fennel, Olive, and Goat Cheese Filling, 158–59, *159*

Hand Pies with Apple, Walnut, and Blue Cheese Filling, 159

Ricotta Tartlets with Celery-Olive Topping, 161

Ricotta Tartlets with Tomato-Basil Topping, *160,* 161

Pineapple, Roasted, Salsa, Chicken-Tomatillo Tacos with, 64–65, *65*

Pistachio

Apricot, and Oat Scones with Garam Masala Glaze, 33

-Crusted Salmon, 96, *97*

Pita Chips, Whole-Wheat

Buttermilk-Ranch, 166

Ras el Hanout, 166

with Salt and Pepper, 166, *167*

Pork

Chop, Barbecue-Rubbed, 82

Chop, Dill-and-Coriander-Rubbed Roasted, 82, *83*

Chop, Herb-Rubbed Roasted, 82

Chop, Roasted Bone-In, with Sweet Potatoes and Maple-Rosemary Sauce, *88,* 89

Chops, Crispy, with Roasted Peach, Blackberry, and Arugula Salad, 84–85, *85*

Chops, Sweet and Spicy Glazed, with Sesame Bok Choy, 86–87, *87*

Make-Ahead Crispy Egg Rolls, 156–57, *157*

Marinated, Gyros, 92–93, *93*

Tenderloin, Lemon-Thyme, with Green Beans and Hazelnuts, 90–91, *91*

see also Ham

Potato(es)

Fans, Crispy Baked, 144, **145**

Roasted, with Parsley, Lemon, and Garlic, *142,* 143

and Mesclun Salad, Roasted Chicken Thighs with, 52–53, *53*

Shoestring Fries, *164,* 165

Shoestring Fries with Coriander and Dill, 165

Shoestring Fries with Rosemary and Lemon Zest, 165

Steak Frites, 78–79, *79*

see also Sweet Potato(es)

Prosciutto-Wrapped Chicken with Cantaloupe-Cucumber Salad, *44,* 45

Q

Quinoa

Overnight Breakfast Grain Bowl, *30,* 31

Overnight Breakfast Three-Grain Bowl, 31

R

Radicchio

and Butternut Squash, Roasted Chicken Sausages with, *66,* 67

and Pear Salad, Make-Ahead Lentil and Mushroom Burgers with, 129

Radishes and Snap Peas, Honey-Glazed Salmon with, 98–99, *99*

Ramekins, 11

Red Curry Chicken Kebabs with Peanut Dipping Sauce, *152,* 153

Romesco, *168,* 169

S

Salads

Asparagus and Citrus, Roasted Swordfish with, 108–9, *109*

Brussels Sprout and Citrus, Chipotle-Honey Fried Chicken with, 50–51, *51*

Salads (*cont.*)

Cantaloupe-Cucumber, Prosciutto-Wrapped Chicken with, *44,* 45

Chicken and Chickpea, with Carrots, Cucumber, and Feta, *60,* 61

Corn and Black Bean, Flank Steak with, *80,* 81

Creamy Apple-Fennel, Crispy Breaded Chicken Breasts with, 42–43, *43*

Hoisin-Ginger Chicken, with Napa Cabbage, Shiitakes, and Bell Pepper, 62–63, *63*

Mango and Cucumber, Ginger-Turmeric Scallops with, 110–11, *111*

Mesclun, and Potatoes, Roasted Chicken Thighs with, 52–53, *53*

Radicchio and Pear, Make-Ahead Lentil and Mushroom Burgers with, 129

Roasted Butternut Squash, with Za'atar and Halloumi, *124,* 125

Roasted Peach, Blackberry, and Arugula, Crispy Pork Chops with, 84–85, *85*

Spicy Roasted Shrimp and Fennel, with Cannellini Beans and Watercress, 112–13, *113*

Vegetable and Bulgur, Spiced Chicken Kebabs with, 58–59, *59*

Salmon

Burgers with Tomato Chutney, 102–3, *103*

Hazelnut-Crusted, 97

Honey-Glazed, with Snap Peas and Radishes, 98–99, *99*

Pistachio-Crusted, 96, *97*

Sesame, with Roasted Kimchi, Broccoli, and Shiitakes, *100,* 101

Smoked Almond–Crusted, 97

Salsa, Roasted Pineapple, Chicken-Tomatillo Tacos with, 64–65, *65*

Sauces

Goat Cheese and Chive, 147

Parsley-Shallot, 78, *79*

Romesco, *168,* 169

Spicy Maple Syrup, 147

Sausages. *See* Chicken Sausages

Scallops, Ginger-Turmeric, with Mango and
Cucumber Salad, 110–11, *111*

Scones

Apricot, Pistachio, and Oat, with Garam
Masala Glaze, 33

Currant, Almond, and Oat, with Earl Grey
Glaze, 33

Make-Ahead Fruit, Nut, and Oat, 32, *33*

Seeds

Date-Almond Snack Bars, *172,* 173

toasting, 12

Shallot(s)

and Carrots, Roasted, Lemon-Sage Top
Sirloin Steak with, *74, 75*

and Cauliflower, Roasted, Coriander
Chicken Thighs with, 56–57, *57*

-Parsley Sauce, 78, *79*

and Thyme, Roasted Mushrooms with,
138, 139

Shellfish. *See* Scallops; Shrimp

Shrimp

with Curry Noodles, 114–15, *115*

and Fennel, Spicy Roasted, Salad with
Cannellini Beans and Watercress,
112–13, *113*

Tacos, Chipotle, *116,* 117

Silicone muffin cups, 11

Skewers, 5, 11

Smoked Almond–Crusted Salmon, 97

Smoked Paprika Chickpeas, Crispy, 170

Snack Bars, Date-Almond, *172,* 173

Soufflé dish, 11

Spatula, nonstick-safe, 11

Spices, toasting, 12

Spinach, Artichokes, and Feta, Baked Eggs
with, 20, *21*

Squash

Butternut, and Radicchio, Roasted
Chicken Sausages with, *66,* 67

Roasted Butternut, Salad with Za'atar and
Halloumi, *124,* 125

Roasted Delicata, *146,* 147

see also Zucchini

Sweet Potato(es)

Hearty Vegetable Hash with Golden
Yogurt, *26,* 27

and Maple-Rosemary Sauce, Roasted
Bone-In Pork Chop with, *88,* 89

Wedges, Roasted, 140, *141*

Swordfish, Roasted, with Asparagus and
Citrus Salad, 108–9, *109*

T

Tacos

Chicken-Tomatillo, with Roasted Pineapple
Salsa, 64–65, *65*

Chipotle Shrimp, *116,* 117

Tahini-Yogurt Dipping Sauce, Beef-and-
Bulgur Meatballs with, 154–55, *155*

Tartlets, Ricotta

with Celery-Olive Topping, 161

with Tomato-Basil Topping, *160,* 161

Toast, Roasted Fruit and Almond Butter,
28, *29*

Toaster ovens with air fryer function, 7

Tofu, Five-Spice and Eggplant, Ramen
Noodle Bowl with, 126–27, *127*

Tomatillo-Chicken Tacos with Roasted
Pineapple Salsa, 64–65, *65*

Tomato(es)

Avocado, and Herb Salad, Egg in a Hole
with, 16, *17*

-Basil Topping, Ricotta Tartlets with,
160, 161

and Charred Green Beans, Spicy Peanut
Chicken with, 48–49, *49*

Chutney, Salmon Burgers with, 102–3, *103*

and Gorgonzola, Roasted Steak Tips with,
72, *73*

and Mushrooms, Roasted, Chicken Thighs
with, *54,* 55

Plum, Roasted, 12

Romesco, *168,* 169

Sauce, Spiced, Orzo, and Feta, Turkey-
Zucchini Meatballs with, 38–39, *39*

Tomato(es) (*cont.*)

Sun-Dried, Broccoli, and Cheddar
Frittata, 23

Tongs, 11

Trail Mix, Almond, Cherry, and Chocolate,
174, *175*

Turkey

Burgers, California, *40,* 41

-Zucchini Meatballs with Orzo, Spiced
Tomato Sauce, and Feta, 38–39, *39*

V

Vegetable(s)

and Bulgur Salad, Spiced Chicken Kebabs
with, 58–59, *59*

Hash, Hearty, with Golden Yogurt, *26,* 27

see also specific vegetables

Y

Yogurt

Golden, Hearty Vegetable Hash with,
26, 27

Sauce, Asparagus Fries with, 162, *163*

-Tahini Dipping Sauce, Beef-and-Bulgur
Meatballs with, 154–55, *155*

Z

Zucchini

Red Pepper, and Bread Hash, Smoky,
Baked Eggs with, *18,* 19

and Shiitakes, Roasted, Top Sirloin Steak
with, 76–77, *77*

-Turkey Meatballs with Orzo, Spiced
Tomato Sauce, and Feta, 38–39, *39*

White Bean and Mushroom Gratin,
122–23, *123*